Moon Spells

Step-by-step Guide to Wiccan Moon Spells

(Channeling Lunar Energy for Spiritual Growth and Manifestation)

Stephen Lozoya

Published By **Chris David**

Stephen Lozoya

All Rights Reserved

Moon Spells: Step-by-step Guide to Wiccan Moon Spells (Channeling Lunar Energy for Spiritual Growth and Manifestation)

ISBN 978-1-7774403-9-8

No part of this guidebook shall be reproduced in any form without permission in writing from the publisher except in the case of brief quotations embodied in critical articles or reviews.

Legal & Disclaimer

The information contained in this book is not designed to replace or take the place of any form of medicine or professional medical advice. The information in this book has been provided for educational & entertainment purposes only.

The information contained in this book has been compiled from sources deemed reliable, and it is accurate to the best of the Author's knowledge; however, the Author cannot guarantee its accuracy and validity and cannot be held liable for any errors or omissions. Changes are periodically made to this book. You must consult your doctor or get professional medical advice before using any of the suggested remedies, techniques, or information in this book.

Upon using the information contained in this book, you agree to hold harmless the Author from and against any damages, costs, and expenses, including any legal fees potentially resulting from the application of any of the information provided by this guide. This disclaimer applies to any damages or injury caused by the use and application, whether directly or indirectly, of any advice or information presented, whether for breach of contract, tort, negligence, personal injury, criminal intent, or under any other cause of action.

You agree to accept all risks of using the information presented inside this book. You need to consult a professional medical practitioner in order to ensure you are both able and healthy enough to participate in this program.

Table Of Contents

Chapter 1: What Is The Moon? 1

Chapter 2: A Moon Circle 16

Chapter 3: Nature, Herbs And Moon Magic 29

Chapter 4: Phases Of The Moon............. 39

Chapter 5: Why And How To Perform Your Spells 45

Chapter 6: Crystals And Gemstones In Moon Magic... 58

Chapter 7: Lunar Magical Enhancement 78

Chapter 8: Spells 87

Chapter 9: What Is Wicca? 119

Chapter 10: World Of Wicca 149

Chapter 11: The Energy Of The Moon .. 152

Chapter 12: The Eight Phases Of The Moon 171

Chapter 1: What Is The Moon?

Moon is among the celestial body. It's, in actual the only natural celestial body that directly connects the earth, and is a source of power which you, as a human who believes in it will access. Some might say that it's only a satellite as per the scientific method, but how off you are! The natural blessing to mankind isn't just a satellite which orbits around Earth, it's a manifestation of a variety of powers that will alter your whole life and turn your most cherished desires to life. The only thing you have to learn is how to harness the energy and power of the moon. However, first you have to know the moon's characteristics before you are able to harness the power of it.

The moon is thought as the energy mother of the universe, while the sun represents the father of energy This is due to the fact that moon energy is linked to feminine energy, flexibility, reflection as well as intuition. The moon also is known to be in close contact with the element water of the earth. Moon's power can be harnessed through its various phases. Knowing the phases is the most important factor in getting the moon's energy for moon-related spells.

People who are deeply into the practices of Wicca (a ritual of magic and nature worship) have also declared that the moon lives within each zodiac sign around two and a half hours as well as affects every person differently, and is related to their particular characteristics. Aren't you interested?

Numerous names have been assigned to the moon by various peoples, which highlights the importance of the moon's body for the people. There are however widespread names in all religions that refer to the moon throughout all twelve months in the calendar.

January: Wolf Moon

This is the very first Full Moon of the calendar; it's an ideal time to let go of anything you believe is weighing your down.

It's it's a time for cleansing yourself to allow to peace within and provide an ideal ground to make fresh beginnings.

February: Snow Moon or Ice Moon

It is the 2nd full moon in the calendar and is referred to as Snow moon for the snow storms that occur in February. This is an extremely harsh time as the ground remains dry and everybody eagerly anticipates the arrival of spring.

The Snow moon enables us to harness the same energy that people of the past had to survive the freezing winter, brutal February. It helps build endurance and strength. Also, it is an ideal time that we are in hibernation. It is an ideal time to examine our own lives and accept responsibility for previous mistakes, and to make amends. It is also and a time to get ready for the coming season.

March: Storm Moon or Worm Moon

The full moon was given the name Worm moon since this is an hour when all glaciers on the earth begins to melt and worms start to emerge from hibernation. It's also the start of a new cycle. It is the perfect time to examine your financial objectives and create the most of those money and luck spells. As it's a time of rebirth, it's important for fertility and wealth So set your goals in line with the time of increase. Be introspective and aware of your own potential and take an inspiration from the awakened self.

April: Growing Moon or Pink Moon

The moon's name comes it was not because the moon changed into a pink hue, rather, it's because of the beautiful flower that blooms in this time which signals the beginning of spring. As it's an time of blossoming and blossoms, it's a time to begin new projects to take chances and take positive steps. It's also an ideal time for healing and healing, it is a time to heal from past wounds and recover the wounds of past trauma, an time to be whole.

May: Milk Moon or Hare Moon

This time in the season the grasses have begun to expand, the animals are starting to feed and production of milk is in full swing. It's true and that's why the term milk moon originated. It's the blooming season which is a time of multiplying so set some objectives for your career and adopt an attitude of growth that will push you towards the direction of growth.

June: Strawberry Moon or Mead Moon

This time it is the time when leaves come fully blooming on trees. Everything is lively and lush. The cool summer breeze is gradually taking over spring. The Strawberry moon symbolizes the vision and dreams; It's a time to reconnect with ourselves and discover the world around us.

July: Hay Moon or Meadow Moon

It's summertime It is the perfect time to unwind, reflect and recharge. Spend the peaceful time by joining a circle. You can also share in the energy of the full moon. It's a great time to make use of the warmth of summer to harvest dried herbs and store them as preparations for the winter.

August: Corn Moon or Red Moon

It is the time that marks the start of the harvest season; we start to reap the bounty we receive from the earth during this time and can take advantage of the bounty from the earth that nourish our bodies as well as our minds.

It is the perfect time to be focused on the goals we have set for health and wellbeing. This is also an ideal time where we are in a state of equilibrium between hope and fear. As this is the start of the harvest season, there is optimism for an abundant harvest, but also the worry that something could go wrong. So we make the work and trust that the universe will reward our efforts.

September: Harvest Moon or Barley Moon

As of now, the harvesting has begun and winter storage starts. The brightness of the moon allows farmers the extra time to gather their harvest until late at night. Also, this is the time when we can ensure that our stocks of fresh herbs will be enough to last us throughout winter. It's a great time to create the goals you want to achieve for your family as well as a time to think about the future.

October: Blood Moon or Hunters Moon

The autumn season is fully underway as the trees lose their leaves. The harvest is over as both humans as well as beasts are stuffed with the bounty of the harvest. It's a time to show our appreciation to the ancestors who gave us the blessing of harvest as well as an enjoyable planting season. be seeking wisdom and guidance for the long-term sustainability of the season of extremes to come.

November: Tree Moon or Snow Moon

When at this time that snow or rain is beginning to fall, and wild animals start to get ready for hibernation. It is an opportunity to take a time to sit and take a step back, it is a time to think about the year that has passed and to be relaxed in the peace and security that from the blessings our past ancestors offers. This is also an ideal time to release the regrets of mistakes that were that we made throughout the course of the year. Also, it is a great time to connect with the calmness this time of year brings to ease our constantly paced lives and shed any negativity that we have about the upcoming winter.

December: Cold Moon/ Oak Moon

The winter chill is settling in and the days are getting longer and more dark today. This is the time to slow down and be in touch with your own spirit, get at one with the seasons and remain still, so you are able to see clearly and vision big. The process of being still also gives us relaxation and helps us get rid of anxiety and stress since with a clear purpose is confidence and optimism. This is the ideal time to record your goals for weight loss, the things you'd like to shed and the habits you wish to shed, the lifestyle that you're planning to build as well as the qualities that you want to achieve.

Supernatural Powers of the Moon

After you have learned more about the moon, we can learn more about the mystical potential it has. The moon acts as the source of power for the realm of the supernatural and the source of energy that drives any magic or ritual can be found in the moon. The moon's energy source is a mystery which could be one of the reasons why its power is so powerful. When it comes to the practices of Wicca it is believed that the moon acts as symbolic because its stages are crucial in determining what magick that is performed each time. Similar to how farmers follow the seasons in advance of plant, so the moon acts as our daily guide life.

Moonlight as an energy source is a great way to recharge elements of the Earth to boost the effectiveness of spells. As an example, there's moon water. Moon water is said to have dissolved the energy of the moon by exposing to it. That is, it is charged by the moon's light. The most common use for moon water is as an addition to spells and rituals for more potency. In some cases, this water is utilized in lieu of the moon's energy to provide the required energy for a moon phase. Moon water can be created during any moon's phase, which means we have the possibility of having moonwater that is new as well as full moon water. the waxing of moon water waxing moon water as well as dark moonwater. They all are created from the energy released by the moon during that particular stage of the moon.

A Time for Spells

After you have mastered the moon's phases and phases, you may be perplexed as to whether the time of week when a spell takes place is important, and the answer is it does and doesn't.

Sure, as long as you perform your spell on the ideal date of the week that is assigned to this spell can add extra flavor to the spell. But it's not because even without that extra spice it's still powerful. The process of synchronizing the correct date and the appropriate lunar phase for the right spell is very difficult, as you could be waiting a few days for a the perfect sync. If you're lucky enough to experience a sync with the moon's phase and day you should take advantage of it. If not you should just focus on the correct time of the moon. The moon's phase is the primary element in moon-related spells.

Appropriate Days for Spells

Sunday: Spells to help clear and direction. Spells to bring completeness in mind and body.

Monday: healing spells, connecting with God Invoking spirits and psychic abilities.

Tuesday: Mindfulness and protection spells, as well as an enhanced sexual drive spell.

Wednesday: A day of advancement could be in the field of academics, careers and business, or in relation to travel schedules.

Thursday: Spells for money spiritual expansion spells, legal issues.

Friday: Romance spells, reconciliation spell, love spell, attraction spells

Saturday: Spells to end unhealthy habits, spells for ending toxic relationships, spells to start new projects.

Locations to Execute Spells

While performing spells, a important element is your. The moon is the main energy of moon magic, however, you're the channel therefore the effectiveness of the spell is dependent upon you. Consequently where you perform the ritual is dependent upon you. Ancient times, most spells were performed outdoors because nature interaction adds an element of spirituality to the ceremonies. But, over the last few years as we have seen the rise of civilization, and an growing activity in cities, the constant noise and buzzing of people; executing outdoors spells have become more improbable. It isn't a good idea to find yourself at the center of your spells only to get stares from people passing by. Or awake the next morning to find your online video as someone spotted you and recorded a video, in the dark, without your knowledge.

It is the reason I mentioned in the past that you're the most important ingredient. If you're in a serene area where you are able to focus and stay fully engaged with the activity this could be the ideal place to let your magic happen. This could include any space in your home that the light of the moon is visible, or it may also be situated within your backyard. One of the main factors to think about before deciding where to put your garden include:

Privacy

The first thing to think about before you decide on the location to cast your spells since it is mandatory to be on your own and not be accompanied by any other person(s) who are part of the ritual or spell in the role of participants.

Comfort

You're the channel consequently your comfort is vitally important.

Quietness

It is important to stay clear of all external distractions, mainly sounds.

Safety

The need for a safe place is crucial so you won't be forced to be while in a state of anxiety.

Wind

If you are planning to use candles for spells It is possible think about the effects on the winds blowing around the candles.

There are exceptions too when your location is not able to receive direct light by the moon. If this is the case it is possible to use an image that is a substitute for the moon or something that resembles the moon for the person you are. Be aware that you're the channel, therefore your beliefs play an important part in this as does the belief of others in the group if you're conducting a group spell.

There are those who believe that spells for groups are more effective in the outside environment; however, that choice is yours to make. So long as the requirements listed above are satisfied, either on or off the ground Moon spells still be powerful in the way they are supposed to be.

While outside rituals have become less real in the present, whenever you can get the chance to retreat to a peaceful space or even a city, don't miss the opportunity to go outside for a moon-spell. It can be like a taste to the experience that you experience when doing rituals or spells.

If space is available the space allows, you could build an altar for permanent use. It's not as difficult as it seems the process of the process of making an altar isn't quite as hard as it appears.

Chapter 2: A Moon Circle

In order to make anything, you must be able to understand the concept behind it. Let's look at the moon's circle.

A moon circle is the gathering of women around an altar in the New moon or Full moon to provide an safe environment to discuss their vulnerabilities, fears growing, experiences and gather energy by performing rituals, meditation, or reciting mantras and more. In order to better understand it the moon circle is similar to an esoteric support group which will nourish the soul.

Moon circles go from the time in which women had to be separated from their communities for their menstrual cycle, that is usually in tune with the lunar cycle. Women would gather with their friends with what is known as the red tents, to enjoy their feminine beauty as well as their spirituality. Also, this is the time in which they focus on enhancing their physical and mental wellbeing. Women who are older who are part of these groups take time to care for and instruct young girls the importance to be whole in the women's lives. As young women enter their first menstrual cycle and are ushered into the tent of red, at which point they're ushered into womenhood, gaining knowledge from seniors and learning how to look after them throughout the time during the period. To celebrate the girls perform rituals of passage, which include blood dripping directly onto the ground, putting on red attire that has red body decorations as well as chanting mantras and celebrating on an altar. It was also during this time in which they uncovered their heritage as a family as well as the power of womanhood.

The present in which there's not much time to escape from your busy life due to menstrual cycles finding a different method to replenish, revive and recharge your body is vitally important. The New moon's cycle serves the purpose. It's a non-judgment area A place in which all have a connection to Sisterhood. Moon circles can serve as a space to talk the burdens of life, to let go and heal. It could be a source to gain insight to the future. Be aware you are able to use the moon circle on your own. There is power when you have a group of people.

Creating a Moon Circle

For setting up a moon-shaped circle, you must adhere to these easy steps:

Select your preferred design

This isn't difficult since moon circles are designed to correspond with the month's sign. Make use of that for a guideline. The addition of gemstones and crystals to the color of the month that are placed on the altar as well an additional flavor for the building of energy. The synchronization of your theme with the month's color creates an empowering power that helps the earth be in alignment with your wishes by aligning your wishes to the energy accessible from the moon at the time. It isn't an absolute requirement. You may still select a subject that meets the desires of those in your circle. After all, your group is supposed to be an enjoyable and healthy space to all who participate, so remember it is all about the participants and you and that is why you should pick something that which you feel comfortable in or something that will add some fun and thrills, as well as make the environment more relaxed and allow everyone to be comfortable.

Some examples of themes that are relatable are:

Self-care

Communication

Letting go

Rebirth

Making plans

Relaxation and rest

Manifestation

Connect to your intuition

Looking for a glimpse in the near future

Looking inward

These are only suggestions to help you understand the best way to design your moon circle. Remember that the subject of a moon-shaped circle is different from that of a full moon's circle since they represent distinct energy sources.

Set up an altar

The most crucial aspect since it is what the circle actually looks like. It is a physical space which acts as a portal into the realm of the spirit. It is where you place things that symbolize your goals or items that represent the kind of energy that you want to access. In general an altar must consist of a minimum of one thing that represents the four directions of the earth. I.e., North, South, East and, West. Every object is also associated to any from the four components that comprise the universe.

North (Earth) All items that originate directly from earth and are connected to the earth. They is possible to use, for example precious gems, stones and plants.

South (Fire): Candles, match sticks

East (Air) (Air): feathers and incense

West (Water) Seashells Pebbles, seashells, water Elixir

It is possible to have the altar personalized by requesting each participant in the circle to donate anything of significance to their altar. Prior to the ceremony every participant puts an item in the center of the altar one by each other. The altar becomes one-of-a-kind and simultaneously, at the at the same time it is a communal channel of energy. It is important to note that moon circles is actually circular, which is the reason for its designation. Perhaps you are wondering why it is it isn't a triangle? This is due to the fact that the energy is more concentrated within a circle. Additionally, because the start of the last of a circle can't be identified, energy is locked in without breaking.

To decorate your altar, you may require specific items based upon your goals, however essential items include:

The Athame, also known as an athame, is a knife that is used during rituals. If you're not comfortable with knives, you could utilize a letter opener. be aware that you must be comfortable with the tools you use. The tool you select for your Athame must be used only for sacred purposes and used only in rituals.

Incense is utilized to create an opening during rituals in order to purify the environment of negativity and create the way to attract positive energy in some situations; also, it acts as a signal to the intentioned supernatural force.

Candles: These are crucial components of rituals because they are the symbol of the fire element and the ceremony will determine what kind of candle should use. The rituals, however, aren't particular about the kind of candle required. In the case of this, you could pick a hue that corresponds to the moon's color and if that's not possible simply pick the colour that you feel drawn by.

Wand: You can go to buy a already-made and enhanced wand or make your own.

Spices and herbs: pick in accordance with the purpose of the moon's circle.

A chalice or a cauldron If a cauldron seems too big, consider another chalice. These can serve as of mixing bowls for mixing incense and herbs, for burning or holding water. They can also be used to store the ingredients needed to perform the ceremonies.

Jewelry could be the form of a talisman or necklace, a ring with a fortified design as well as a rosary. anything else that will give you a sense of awe when it is worn. You could also have jewellery passed down to you via the lineage of your ancestors.

Tree extracts and plant plants Choose depending on the intentions of your moon's orbit.

Crystals and rocks: choose depending on the meaning of the moon's circling.

Other items that could be incorporated into the altar could be Tarot cards, cash or a device you utilize for work, mirrors photographs e.t.c. As I have said in the ritual, the comfort of your circle participants is a top priority. Why would you want to be doing a ritual in the presence of people who are hesitant regarding your setup? The power of a circle lies because of its unity.

Make a circle.

The opening ceremony is a part of the ritual and is typically performed to seal the circle and seal in the energy. The ritual of opening acts as a grounding point for the group and draws all participants to the realization that they're inside a sacred place. The open ceremony also includes being aware that what is that is said or shared within the circle is holy and must not, in any way use as a weapon against anyone else. The circle is emphasized as an inclusive and safe place to be in.

This is an example of beginning ritual that involves all the participants sitting around the altar, you could invite everyone to hold a lit candle or light an incense at the altar to rid the space of any negative energy. Then, the person who hosts the circle will lead the group in the chant of grounding or an enthralling mantra or meditation while the group holds hands. Once the chanting or meditation is completed, it's time for the bare-faced moment. This is where each participant introduces the other. Once the opening of the circle has been completed, you are able to begin to discuss the goal of the circle in a proper manner.

Setting intentions and sharing

At this point, lead everyone to the purpose of this moon circle. The focus of the group is engaged. The floor is now open to a moment of silence in which everyone is able to share their thoughts without feeling considered a failure. Following the sharing, it's time to make plans and be accountable, as it's similar to telling your circle of your friends about the goals you've made up the intention to reach in regards to aspects of your health. If you discuss your goals to people with energy that is positive, it helps build resolution and focus; the universe is also listening and initiates an aid system to guide you towards achieving the goals you have set. The first stage in the circle is an important point because it builds a sense of an atmosphere of connection between all participants. This creates a connection as well as a safe environment that provides room for vulnerability, openness and determination.

Moon Channeling

It is a time when the power of the moon can be used to charge our souls. The full or new moon ritual takes place during this time in accordance with the circle is it. This ceremony is connected to the purpose that the circles are forming. Let's say the purpose of the circle is rest and Relaxation. If so the calming ritual or spell is performed to nourish your spirit with moon's energy. This will then work in accordance with your goals and bring these to fruition by relaxing the mind and helping to ease tension. It can also be utilized to recharge the tools you use, such as crystals and water, and to sharpen your brain the body, your soul and mind. A circle could take an hour of silence to allow members to take a moment for journaling, too.

Closing the Circle

In order to close the circle the closing ceremony is performed. As the energy within circles is ground you shouldn't walk out of the circle quickly it is necessary to design an exit path where each participant can go out one at a time one. This allows the energy to gradually disperse. In order to conclude the ceremony the participants can say the name of their choice, repeating the intention, and go out one by one.

Chapter 3: Nature, Herbs And Moon Magic

Herbs connect us to the earth. They embody all the power that the earth has to offer. When it comes to magic, herbs are essential in the enhancement of the spell, or helping to ground the power of the spell. It is common to use them as a stand-alone supplement to the moon since they can be very powerful by themselves. If you are using herbs for spells, it is carefully to ensure the safety of the herb before taking it the herb, particularly when making your spell. Otherwise, adhere to the tested and reliable guidelines. A few of the herbs mentioned have powerful magical properties within them. Use be cautious; if you're not confident about making use of one particular herb don't include it in your spell, opt for a different one that which you're certain of.

Many kinds of herbs are utilized in the realm of magic. It is impossible to list every single one of them in this section. Other journals are that are dedicated to the use of herbs. In them, you will be able to learn about the many varieties of herbs as well as how you can use these.

Here are a few instances of herbs that are natural that are used for various purposes;

Beet

It can be used as a replacement for blood in spells. It is used to make ink to write love spells. It's also a herb for love.

Barley

As a component for healing, love and protection spells. In order to protect yourself from harm Sprinkle it on the area. If you're hurting, attach the stone to it and drop it into the water. This can help relieve your pain.

Banana

To increase your prosperity, power and fertility spells.

Banyan

In order to attract luck and the joy of life

Basil

Afflicting fear on hostile spirits can be employed to draw in money as well as dispel fears, weakness and disorientation.

Bay leaf

It's a herb that purifies that provides protection, healing and psychic abilities. The herb is also utilized to create good fortune spells. Also, it is utilized in protection spells to combat black magic.

Carrot

Enhances the desire for sexual activity and fertility, particularly when you are in search of the child born.

Cabbage

The perfect choice for lunar spells brings good luck good fortune, prosperity, as well as fertility

Coconut

To strengthen chastity, strengthening cleansing and protecting

Clove

to attract wealth, protection and affection. Additionally, it is used for the practice of exorcism.

Corn

The use of this stone is for luck, protection, and divination spells. The talisman can be placed on the wall to ward off negative luck.

Blood of the Dragon

The most effective method to utilize this herb is to ignite the incense as an incense. it smothers negative energy and cleans the surrounding area. it is also used as a part of waning moon spells to assist in getting rid of bad habits or getting rid of a bad relationship. Certain spells is utilized to remove impermanence.

Epsom salt

Commonly, it is used to make ritual baths.

Eucalyptus

This plant is gold in the realm of magic. It is employed in its dried form for stuffing into healers' puppets, sachets, and pillows. Also, it can be used to provide healing vibrations, and is mainly utilized as a purifier. It's also used in reconciliation spells and healing spells.

Fig

A lot of people use it for love spells and fertility. It's also used in divination spells, too.

Flaxseed

In spells to protect and prosperity in material terms. Place some in your wallet or purse, or in your pocket will help you avoid poverty.

Garlic

Most often, it is used for exorcism. It is also used to remove negative and evil spirits, as well as in healing spells.

Ginger

Enhancing sexual desire and confidence. It also promotes prosperity and success. It strengthens any mixture it's included in, which is why it acts as an boost in energy and potency. Also, it can be utilized to strengthen Athames as well as blades that are used during rituals. The ginger root also has a shape with a human shape. The humans-like ginger roots can be exceptionally powerful and may represent an actual being.

Magnolia

It is useful in spells for stopping routines. Inspiring harmony between lovers, enhancing fidelity dedication, health, improving the beauty of your life, tranquility and calmness when you are stressed.

Maple syrup

Spells for love, money as well as longevity spells. prosperity generally.

Mustard seeds

Mustard seed is among the oldest talismans for luck found in the magick. The seed is commonly used in the creation of Voudoun Charms. to increase faith and courage.

Oak

The oak is the largest and most vital tree for the practice of Wicca The entire structure of this tree has power all the way from the leaf up to the bark, and finally the root. The oak is a mighty tree, which is useful for almost any magick. It is utilized in crafting tools for magic, and leaves are used to cleanse and strengthen.

Orchid

Useful in spells to help develop a excellent memory, sharp mind with a strong determination, an unwavering concentration.

Pink root

For healing spells.

Pink Rosebud

As a base for magic spells for love, so that once buds grow, relationship will be strengthened.

Plum

To get love spells, as well as a calm and peaceful environment.

Primrose

It encourages the discovery of the truth. It also uncovering hidden truths as well as unravelling some of the mysteries.

Radish

To protect and lust.

Rye

Self-control spells as well as fidelity spells, love spells.

Sage

Purification rituals are used to purify self-purification, in consolation spells to assist with grieving for loss Mental health spells, techniques to enhance the brain. It improves overall well-being which includes physical, mental and spiritual health. It's also used to aid in the longevity spells. It's also crucial to keep in mind that sage attracts negative energy as well as misfortunes Don't let used sage around the house Instead, put it in a secluded area. Also, it is a bad idea to cultivate sage within your garden so to avoid this, it is possible to solicit help from someone else to plant it so that the plant isn't yours to do it in the first place. Also, when you plant sage, make sure to plant it next to the other plants so that it's tendency to elude negative energy can be neutralized.

Turnip

Utilized in the waning moon spells to end connections.

Tulip

Brings happiness, love as well as delight and protection. The colour of Tulip is a good choice to be selected to correspond with the subject of the ritual.

Vervain

The herb is known as holy or witch's plant. It's generally the best herb for every magick. It's used in the protection of spells to create a calm and peaceful environment, it stimulates the need to learn and developing wisdom. It can also bring positive dreams, and also helps to ease anxiety. If you're performing rituals in honour of a god from the past it is possible to use vervain. When performing such rituals they are appropriate time is the night of the night. Vervain can also be used as jewelry and also as a talisman. There is also a general belief from folklore that vervain is an Achilles' heel for vampires.

Chapter 4: Phases Of The Moon

Imagine yourself in the driving seat of your life. Are you not drowning in constant confusion of what to do next? Being a part of people who go every day tormented caused by constant despair and discontent. Imagine the complete satisfaction that you will gain from this! Knowing the phases of the moon can aid you to achieve this by making use of the power each of the moon's phase provides as a trigger for your casting spells.

Five phases are present in the moon. These stages are the many shapes that the moon adopts as it circles the earth These phases are triggered depending on the light that the moon provides each time.

Let's now look at the different phases of this natural symbol of power known as moon.

New Moon

This is akin to the resurrection that the moon has. This is the initial glimpse of the moon following the darkness of the night. It's an ideal time for new beginnings. the first crescent light can be visible following the moon's in darkness for two or three days. The moon's new phase is an ideal time to establish objectives, set your sights and prepare your brain to accept that dream that you've always longed for. Clear the clutter in your life, think about how you can gain momentum to achieve that romantic relationship you've always wanted with your partner Perhaps it's a flourishing enterprise that you want to start or even a new job. this is the time to prepare for action. Did you know that it was the ideal time to begin a new romantic relationship? It's now clear! This is the best time to say an love spell.

Waxing Moon

The moon phase is in which the moon waxes more powerful; it is revealing its true form. As a result, it's bigger and brighter. This means that the energy that can be connected to it is greater and stronger. Think of it as a bulb that was covered and now has its appearance almost visible to reveal its glow and the elements around it would be able to feel the power that it emits. It is the exact way that the moon's waxing phase has more powerful effect on spells that are that are being performed in this time. It's the time to take the action. Go job searching Make that phone appointment with that huge client that you'd like to capture. This time all is clearer. The choice of the best spell to suit the needs of your current situation could alter your life for the better.

Full Moon

It is a time where emotions can be heightened and the power from the moon high in this time This is the best time for any type of magic spell. In this time there is a chance for everything to be larger, and everything is possible to accomplish! We can use the example of a bulb in order to see a more clear picture. Imagine the light bulb completely visible without obstacles whatsoever, and the entire area surrounding the bulb experiencing the full force from the brightness of the light bulb. Yes! It's that picture. The maximum impact of the moon's energies can be seen in magical spells during the full moon. If you're a psychic, you'll notice the abilities you have are enhanced during this time and it's almost as if the clarity that you experience that is clear without blur!

Waning Moon

In this particular phase that the moon has slowed down becoming darker and more than it appears to be taking a step back. It is the time to harness this energy that is withdrawn from the moon. Break patterns, break free from an unhealthy relationship and forget about a difficult incident, or end the divorce without a hard sensation or begin an entirely new eating plan. This is the time of giving up.

Dark Moon

It is a time when the moon is absent out of the sky for between 2 and three days. It is an ideal time in which you are at peace and it is a time to contemplate, think and do lots of soul-searching, introspection as well as reorganizing your thoughts and the way you live your life total. Simply put, it is the ideal time to get rid of the waste and purify yourself from the inside.

Moon phases take place monthly, which means the moon goes through a full cycle throughout the month. To be exact, a complete lunar cycle takes place every 29 and a half days. The reason for this is that the moon that falls in each month is named different due to the fact that there's a new moon and the full moon each month. It is one rare occasion when there two full moons within an entire month, due to the lunar days cycle. The second full moon which happens within a month is known as"the Blue moon.

Lunar Calendar

It refers to what is the time it takes the moon to complete its whole cycle of one full moon and then another full moon. This process takes 29 and a half hours, beginning with the full moon, and concluding by the dark moon.

Chapter 5: Why And How To Perform Your Spells

Why?

Some people wonder: why engage in rituals and spells why do we need to engage in rituals and spells?' in the end, There are many individuals who live their lives and do well without the assistance from the divine or understanding of the subject. It's true. You can certainly navigate life without practice of rituals or spells and be successful, but being being attuned to your soul's inner voice increases the clarity of your mind, increases your ability to discern and improves the degree of self-awareness. If you are asking why for some of us the reason we are involved in rituals, we are calling our soul and sifting deep to draw the energy it, with the other tools offered by nature to act as catalysts that help us stand in the void and move us out of a state where struggle towards a higher level and peace within. In particular, there times when you feel overwhelmed, confused and are unable to put everything together. Relaxing seems to be some strange thing, however an easy relaxation routine can bring you back to calm in a short time then you'll be able to go back to your drawing page and complete your tasks without a haze of confusion.

When you use spells, you call upon the power from the universe to your advantage. This triggers the various forces that help bring your dream to your doorstep. What is the process behind this how do you make it happen? it is possible to wonder. This is the problem: while you are performing rituals, by reciting spells as well as the consciousness of the materials and ingredients used in the process the senses of your body are focused at the moment which you're involved in. since your entire senses are focused on one thing. You're taken to a state that is trance-like, an area of greater energies. What is higher energy to do with reaching your goal? Everything! Keep in mind the phrase: "you can achieve whatever you put your heart and mind to do." Exactly! In the absence of spiritual guidance you can accomplish the most amazing feat simply by being focused. Now imagine your concentration being increased, and with no hesitation, and supported by the power of the universe working as a catalyst. you're getting the idea.

You'd be correct in saying that there is no need for assistance from the spiritual realm through spells and rituals, but everybody needs help and guidance. Why do it all on your own to have the universe help you by providing enormous power?

How?

Techniques for casting spells or engaging in rituals differs. The type of spell you intend to cast will be the determining factor in your technique, tools as well as the ingredients required for casting the spell. So the first thing to think about is the spell you wish to cast as well as the goal you wish it to accomplish.

Steps To Take Before Performing a Spell

Preparation

The process will lead to the time when the ceremony takes place. Be calm as it's not as much of an issue. The preparation includes:

Obtaining the equipment as well as the necessary ingredients to cast the magic.

Purifying them when needed in the course of the procedure.

Choosing the location of your choice and

Ensure you have a date that is secure without issues with interruptions caused by guests who are not expected.

Also, you must be sure that you will have plenty of time for the procedure without interruptions. Think of it as how you are preparing for an important occasion, like something like a gala or a corporate presentation, or even an evening out. Perhaps a date night with the cute lover of yours who you've had your eye for so long! How would you prepare for the date is to choose the perfect attire, select the appropriate place, style the hair and make sure you arrange your agenda throughout the night pre-planning to ensure there is nothing that goes wrong. This is the type of effort you invest in the preparation for your spell's performance in order to make sure the ceremony goes without a hitch. For the actual performance of the spell, it is essential to maintain manners. Your mind must remain in a state of relaxation to allow you to concentrate while doing the ceremony.

Performance

It is the way to carry out the ceremony in the correct way. Begin with a clean slate and wash your body before starting. Make sure you arrange your ingredients in the structure needed to cast your spell. Formations are the places that your spell will be solidly anchored; to put the concept in a simpler way this is the earth's energy anchor that will hold your spell. They can be either single or double strengthened. A good example of a single shape is drawing a circle in a pattern, whereas the double-fortified form includes a different shape inside the circle. Whatever you decide to use, be sure that you feel relaxed. Like we've seen earlier, comfort is an essential element in the success of any type of magic. The soothing music can be played on the background, to help you stay relaxed and you could opt to be completely silent, which suits your needs. Once everything is in place start the process of performing the ritual by sketching the pattern as instructed by the spell. Also, the location of your equipment is dependent on the directions that is given to you to you by the spell. After your ritual is completed and you are ready to seal it in, begin the practice of visualization, which involves you contemplating and visualizing your self surrounded by the light and power of the moon. You will be free from any negative energy or obstacle or discord that might hinder your dreams from to be fulfilled. When you sense a pull to your heart, this is when you feel the connection between your soul and Then begin to cast your spell. After you've completed performing your spell, take a moment to take a moment to absorb the magic and take in all the positive energy that is in the air. Afterwards, you must close your spell then extinguish your incense and candles and then return equipment used to be stored in a safe and secure location.

Tips on Casting Formation

When you are casting any kind of pattern, it could be made using visible tools like pebbles, salt candles, seashells, stones, e.t.c as well as by creating circles in the air.

If choosing the option salt is the popular choice since it symbolizes the enhancement of purification and preservation.

It is important to ensure you keep everything on when casting your form because leaving the formation once it has been cast isn't suggested.

In the event that you must go out of the circle at any time then don't simply leave and get out. Open the circle to create a way that allows you to exit. It is accomplished by placing your first and second fingers of your left hand across the area around you while swiping your fingers to create an opening that you can traverse, and then as you step across the circle. Once you're done and close the circle quickly in the same way.

If you depart from your group during an event, ensure that you return as quickly as possible, since the power of the ritual will be lost during your absence as you're the conduit.

Be careful not to step over your own formation. Always step over it.

Draw your circle clockwise.

After your ceremony is complete, let the energy generated in the ritual by putting your hands together in a prayer-like posture, and slowly opening the space and then declare it done.

Finding Time

Because performing spells requires alone time, finding the time in solitude isn't easy, particularly in the case of marriage with kids, live with parents, or live in the same space that's always full of other people. If you live on your own and have no privacy issues, it's not a difficulty; rather, the issue is their busy schedules in current days when life is so fast-paced and individuals are having to balance work as well as schooling. While at home working while taking care of their family at home, and ending in the evening exhausted, and exhausted to be doing anything else that sleep It is crucial to discuss how you can make time.

Learn what will work your best. If you have to create an action plan as well as replace a pastime by taking the time to indulge in your passion and enjoy yourself, then absolutely, make it happen. It is possible sacrifice some of your hobbies to benefit the community. It is important to realize that the spell should not be done in a hurry. From the initial preparation that leads to the principal performance is essential as your brain must be ready and prepared to provide a source of energy so that your spells can be powerful. This is why the necessity of having the perfect environment as well as time can't be understated. Spells aren't an activity you perform when you're at the bathroom It takes time. An average spell could take 30-45 minutes to an hour. It could take longer if your intention is to sit down for a few minutes to absorb the power and energize your soul. That's why it's important to emphasize the importance of having a proper plan of your schedule in preparation to the day that you plan to cast the spell.

It can also help to be part of groups that share the same interests as yours. The pandemic of the past made us aware of an entirely new approach to life and living, joining communities has become a much easier task. You can opt to join a online group or search for nearby ones to get to know each other better.

Resolving Problems A lot of people encounter the difficulty of coping with criticisms particularly from those around them who don't share the same beliefs as their beliefs regarding the use of spells. The result can be a variety of issues, ranging from minor issues to disagreements that are irreconcilable. This is why it's important to discuss how we can deal with these issues if and when they occur.

In time there's been a variety of doubts and debates regarding the use of Wicca perhaps because the stories of witches who are evil were passed on through generations. There have been references to them in films, books and even in folklore. Certain religions say that casting spells can be a way to feed the Satan. There is no question that dark magick exists however, the majority of spells are non-harmful and intended to improve your awareness of yourself and channel your own energies, and not to force others do something that are against their wishes or hurt the person. It can also be very difficult explaining this concept to someone who aren't eager to understand this practice. Thus, I recommend that you practice your rituals in a quiet manner and do not engage in a debate or argument against someone who doesn't share the beliefs you hold and look at the ritual with a sneer.

Keep in mind that you're the most important factor; if fighting with yourself due to the beliefs you hold and beliefs, put a stop until you've got the peace of mind and have a solid conviction.

It is due to the fact that in order when casting spells, you have to focus on a single mind. It is advised for those with partners to stay at the same level and with their partner prior to performing; this will help keep your union from being a mess when your spouse is not a fan of the method. It is sometimes necessary to allow individuals time to consider the implications and think about them over a period of time. It is possible that they will change their minds at some point. Whatever you take, don't force the beliefs of others to defend the truth. What's the point of arguing when that your goal isn't to please everyone but rather to become a better version of your self.

Chapter 6: Crystals And Gemstones In Moon Magic

In addition to having the ability to transmit waves, as we see in our watches, they're highly effective tools in metaphysics and are used for helping us concentrate and direct our energies towards what we want to accomplish while casting rituals. They function as energy storage that are charged by the moon. They can also be used to heal. abilities. The hue of the gemstones or crystals you choose to utilize will be determined by the type of spell you plan to cast, much like candles. If you can't discover the desired color the crystals of clear quartz make excellent substitutes that can be used in any colour. This instrument is in large part dependent on our senses and so, when choosing the stone you want to use, rub it lightly and let your senses determine if this is the one for you or not. If it feels like it's right for you, it is that perfect stone.

There is a vast array of uses for crystals which we are unable to cover in this volume.

Here are some examples of crystals, and the uses they have:

Clear quartz crystal

It promotes healing, enhances psychic capabilities, and can replicate its functions as any other gemstone.

Moonstone

It enhances psychic powers and this is the reason it got its name. it's the stone of witches.

Malachite

The herb was extensively used during the ancient times to protect against the evil eye. Also, it is an energy boost when used in spells.

Amethyst

Stones used since ancient times by healers and psychics to ease anxiety and rage It also assists in giving us clarity in times of feeling everywhere and uncertain

Turquoise

It is famous for its ability to absorb negative energy as well as providing security. It's also utilized in spells to increase strength.

Charging Your Crystal

Crystal can't be bought and then used right away; they need to be prepared prior to use before. The preparation includes cleansing the crystal, charging it and then making adjustments to the crystal.

Cleansing

It is the procedure of cleansing your crystal of negative energy of persons who have the crystal before you chose the crystal. Cleansing your crystal is done by cleansing the crystal using cool water or simply leaving the crystal in cold water over night.

Charging

The process involves charging crystals under the energy that is the moon. Crystals are charged by the light of the moon's new phase or when the moon is full. Charges under the new moon will give the crystal power to assist in revival, faith and enhance. The full moon, it energizes your crystal to help you achieve whatever it is that you desire to accomplish. That is why the full moon is your most popular choice to charge your crystal.

Tuning

It involves tuning the crystal in the direction you would like to accomplish. You do this by putting the crystal with your hands You can either sit down or sit down. Focus your attention on the frequency of energy you wish to attain. Imagine your dream and the end goal. Do not think about how it will come to becoming a reality; instead, focus solely on the end objective. If, for instance, your aim is to have an enterprise worth billions of dollars imagine yourself managing this business now, and do not fret about the way it could be accomplished, attention to the final objective.

After these three phases are completed, you may utilize your crystal in your next ritual or spell.

Moon Magic and Candles

Candles are essential to the creation of magic since they are the instrument used to illuminate the area and ward off dark energy. They vary in their dimensions, color and the scent. The scent of the candle may not be important when it comes to performing spells, its hue is vital because the color of the candle will determine the type of vibration that it emits, certain spells require particular candle colors associated with their spells.

White Candle

It enhances the effectiveness of the candle employed to. It is used to purify, completeness in the sense of calm, peace and psychic abilities.

Pink Candle

The love of a heart, sensitivity, affectionate relationship.

Brown Candle

The stability of your surroundings, the telepathy you can use and security of your surroundings.

Red Candle

The qualities of fertility, sensitivity, and courage and determination.

Yellow Candle

Wholeness, confidence, attraction.

Green Candle

The success in business and career is a way to counter jealousy towards yourself.

Silver Candle

Disarms negative energy.

Black Candle

Contrary to what many believe this remedy does not incite negative energy. Instead, it blocks negativity.

Blue Candle

Loyalty, protection, serenity, inner calm, fidelity

Orange Candle

A boost of energy, self-control

Purple Candle

Insight, wisdom Sharpening psychic skills.

White candles can be used for situations where the desired color is not readily available. One important thing to consider is the candle's dimensions and the fact that you don't want to have your candle to burn all over your ceremony.

Executing Moon Magic Spells

The most important thing to know what spells to cast in which phase of moonlight is knowing what the purpose of the phases are. When you have this knowledge understanding the phases, knowing when you should perform your spells becomes a snap. Here is a few examples that can help you understand.

New Moon Spells

The moon's new phase is associated with the new and renewed. Examples of moon-related spells are:

Health and vitality in a vibrant way

Wellbeing

Happiness

Vibrant love life

Find a soul mate

Career arcs (starting the business of your choice or searching for an employment)

Pregnancy and labor can be stressful.

Waxing Moon Spells

The moon's waxing phase is associated to growth and expansion.

Vital health

Wellbeing

Happiness

Vibrant love life

Sexual vitality

Career is a term used to describe (starting an enterprise or looking for an employment)

A pay rise or promotion

Fertility

Pregnancy and labor can be stressful.

Spiritual development

Spiritual messages

Foresight

Full Moon Spells

The full moon is associated with full strength and capacity, complete maturation, and heightened perceptions

Inviting a person to a relationship

The search for a soulmate

The connection with the spirit of an unloved one who has passed away.

Vibrant love life

Sexual vitality

Fertility

Spiritual development

Foresight

Group spells

Waning Moon Spells

The moon's waning phase is associated with withdrawal and pulling away. It is also a sign of reducing.

Stopping harmful habits

Anger control

Stopping the addiction

Beating fears

The process of moving on from a break-up

Recovering from injuries

Dark Phase Spells

The dark period is associated with reflection and self-reflection as well as it is a time that cleanses and clears your body and mind of all things that don't nourish it.

Refraining from habitual bad behavior

Anger control

Stopping the addiction

Beating fears

Removing yourself from a romantic love affair

Recovering from injuries

The release of guilt

Lunar Lore and Literacy

Lunar lore simply means lunar folklore. Lunar folklore is said to be living memories of events that were lived with the eyes of awe that is derived from the mystical power that the moon has. These are the beliefs and practices associated with the moon our forefathers have experienced and then passed on for us to use through our lives. Some are outright exaggerations and tall stories for the purpose of scaring children or provide entertainment (which is a common practice by the industry of film; such as the tale of the werewolf as well as the myth of the moon's fullness) Many of them are true and serve as the basis for our understanding about the power moon has, as demonstrated by our ancient ancestors. Through these moon-related stories we can learn about the importance of the moon as well as its role in our lives as a bridge between the spiritual and physical reality. The moon was a source of inspiration for the ancient times. mythology was shared by farmers for the relationship that the moon's phases have to time and seasons. These tales about the best time to cultivate, harvest, construct the foundation, build, castrate, wean or go hunting or fish. The moon-related lores include:

Weaning should never be performed while the moon is at its lowest.

Removal and castrating of animal horns should be performed during the waning of the moon in order to minimize bleeding.

Crab and shrimping are most effective at night.

Animal slaughtering for meat must be conducted at when the moon is at its highest to get better meat.

The days between new moons and full moons are among the most ideal times for catching a large catch for an angler.

If fences are trimmed during the moon's waning and dry phases the fences stay straighter and maintain their bulk and strength.

The best time to mat is the waxing or full moon to ensure healthy and vibrant offspring.

A halo surrounding the moon is a sign of that bad weather is coming.

If Christmas fell at the full moon of the year to come, you could yield a plentiful harvest. The same is true as a moon that is waxing.

There are some cultures that believe that on the fifth day of the full moon, is the time to attempt to have a baby, and the ideal time to test your divination skills is when there's a full moon.

The Lunar Eclipse

An eclipse of the moon occurs as the moon moves into the shadow of earth. It may be total or partial eclipse.

A lunar eclipse that is total occurs an event that occurs when the earth, sun and moon are in complete alignment. A partial lunar eclipse takes place when the alignment is only partial. In order for a lunar eclipse to occur, two requirements that are in order and firstly the planet's body the earth must be between the sun and moon. The moon also has been in full phase.

The lunar eclipse for those of the practitioners of magick is an metaphysical prize because of the additional energy that is at our disposal to carry out the rituals and spells we practice. The rituals performed during this time are typically 4 times more powerful than those performed during normal full moon conditions. As we've already seen, the energy of a full moon in itself is very powerful. Now you know why it is referred to as an energy-rich jackpot. As a novice it is important to be cautious when dealing with the power of this kind of energy. which is the reason why some think that beginners are not allowed to do lunar eclipses. Even though their points are valid but you shouldn't be averse to the chance simply because you're a novice. If nature is going to give us this chance take advantage of it. The most crucial thing to remember is to make sure your centre is grounded properly, so you are not hindering the rituals on your own because it is an enormous amount of energy. It is crucial, and should you not be able to figure out the best way to harness energy at the core of your form then it is suggested to put off your attempts at lunar eclipse rituals until you've learned it correctly. Moonlight is an opportunity to harness energy and dramatically alter our lives, and it is not a good idea to miss the opportunity.

Here are a few examples of rituals and spells you are able to use during the lunar eclipse.

Meditation ritual

cleansing bath

Clarity and goals spell

Charge crystals

Honoring moon gods and offering sacrifices

spells designed to enhance your abilities to read, increase knowledge and insight

connecting in the realm of spirituality, and connecting with your the lost loved ones

Healing spells, rituals, and ceremonies for fertility and reproduction

There is no limit to the possibilities. you could even create moon-lit water for the lunar eclipse that reflects the energy of the eclipse and could be used when the eclipse has ended to serve a variety of uses. For making eclipse water, follow these steps:

1. Find a container that will accommodate the amount of water you wish to keep; be sure to put on lids to help keep the water in good condition when it's being stored.

2. You can fill it up with pure water, if you plan to consume the water. In other cases, rain water creates a natural vibration to your ritual, and you may choose to cover it up or open it up as the power of the eclipse will remain in the air.

3. Set the jar so that it is directly beneath the moon's shadow. If you are able to go outdoors then great. If not, simply locate a suitable spot which is within your home.

4. Make your intentions clear for the water. Say prayers or sing a prayer reciting your

goals. To get extra charged water you can place the crystal in your container.

5. Keep it open until eclipse has passed and when the eclipse has passed, open the container up and keep it in storage in case you need it later.

Blue Moon

Blue moons are the 2nd full moon that occurs within the same month of the calendar. Did you ever hear the expression, "Once in a blue moon"?"

This is actually the moon in which this phrase originated from literally. This is due to the fact that an appearance like this kind moon occurs about every two years. The blue moon is unique since it has twice the strength of a regular full moon. Imagine the power that you receive from a normal full moon being multiplied, increasing the energy of your spell to twice the power! This is the ideal time to cast your spell to reap long-lasting results since the the blue moon's energy thought to be sufficient to render the spell or wishes made with it powerful until it's next moon! The blue moon is not a fool; it's time to plan for the moon to take the most of this amazing source of energy you can harness to flourish and succeed. Unfortunately accessing this incredible energy is only possible each two and a half years. However, it's worth it if you are interested in me. Much like the power that comes from the lunar eclipse it could be overwhelming make sure you are cautious when utilizing the energy for spells and rituals.

Also, you can conserve the energy of the moon's blue light with blue moon water by following the exact same steps above. this time you just need to put the water out for the night.

One tip to remember: When setting your intentions to drink lunar eclipse waters blue moon water other moon water, make your goals in accordance with the month that it falls within. The alignment of this kind creates an even stronger incentive that allows the universe to work for our benefit and meet our desires.

Chapter 7: Lunar Magical Enhancement

These are the methods and actions to consider to help you strengthen and increase the power of your abilities. It all starts with you, and the preparation for yourself as the vessel. The preparations you make can be the basis for the way in which your ritual will be carried out. Like a tiny bit of dirt on your food will render it unpalatable the manner in which you set yourself up prior to the ceremony can enhance the magical powers or make it ineffective. It could be as easy as the clothes you put on and the food you consume and the mental state you are in prior to and following the ceremony.

Let's begin with the fundamental basics: what to wear and what food to have.

What to Wear

Consider comfort Consider comfort; you don't wish to feel uncomfortable or irritable during your period, so choose wearing an open-fit and something that you can lie down, sit or even move with ease in. Cotton is an excellent fabric for you to look at since it's breathable and soft on skin. Thus, when performing rituals it can require time so take this in your mind, and pick one that you could sit for an extended period of time within and feel extremely comfortable. It is also possible to choose clothing that matches the colour of the moon's color at the moment. It will match with candles as well as the moon. If not, go with the color white that symbolizes the purity of wholeness, totality and positivity. If the environment is conducive the option, the best alternative is to dress in the birthday outfit of your choice - exactly simply as you are. If you choose the naked option, make sure that your celebrations are in a quiet area, so your neighbors aren't going to harass the party. In addition, the attire you wear has to be clean and fresh. Ideally, you should have freshly washed.

What to Eat

The reason you wouldn't consume a lot of foods prior to an important interview. This just like eating heavy meals isn't recommended prior to performing your ritual so that you do not sleep off or have to go to the bathroom at the end of your flurry. Thus, consider some light food; if possible, you should do it before eating. If you are forced to consume eating meat. Choose fresh fish that has been cooked, consume moderately, and rest for around an hour prior to begin your routine. An alternative is tea. There is many calming organic teas that you can pick from.

Then, there are the most fundamental that are the condition of your mental state and the peace of your surroundings.

The State of Your Mind

However strong the equipment and other ingredients used in the ritual the ritual will have no value and be a loss of time and equipment when your thoughts are not on the right track. The most important thing your magick requires is your own mind. Get rid of all anxiety, stress, or worry and concentrate on positivity as well as your goals and feel happy for the gifts of the moon as well as its power to us, for growth and overall health. In order to help you enter your state of being ready make sure you take a pre-requisite bath prior to starting.

In your bath, recite these phrases:

"I get rid of all negative thoughts; I give my body positive energy.

I cleanse negativity off my body and allow room to receive positive energy

I am cleansed in and out."

After bathing, put on your bathing suit and prepare for the routine.

After the ritual, your condition of your mind after the ritual is just as crucial as the state of your mind following the ritual. Make sure you keep your thoughts focused and positive upon your goal, even with or without magick. A positive mind accomplishes its goals. and now you can add magick to the equation to double-enforcement. Keep that energy positive regardless of when the ritual is finished and the magick is complete.

The Ambiance of Your Surroundings

An excellent way to set the mood for any event is with a good, appropriate tune. Music, as they say, is a source of nourishment for your soul. Therefore, take care to nourish your soul, and set the mood with classic or an chant, or a music that evokes the nature sounds could also help you get a feeling of being in nature. it adds an additional enchanting experience to your surroundings. Whatever sound you choose to use be sure that it's delicate and smooth with a consistent the rhythm all through; you do not need something to impede or disrupt your journey from the physical world to the spiritual realm. Neither would you like a song which abruptly stops even though you're performing the ritual, or perhaps within a state of Trance. You can imagine yourself having the beauty of a conversation while when you are in the state of trance, and then being jolted back to your physical half when the environment suddenly altered! Terrible right? Absolutely, I do. Thus, try to avoid the likelihood of this happening, and head on a long-distance track.

Tips:

1. A spell may be modified according to your preferences and your needs. If you're not comfortable with the equipment and ingredients modify them to fit you. Always remember comfort is the most important factor.

2. If you don't have all the colors mentioned in the spell, you are able to use any other color to replace white.

3. Clear quartz is a good substitute.

4. To add fragrance, lavender could replace any scent.

Tools of the Trade

These are the equipment and substances used during the procedure of carrying out the ritual. They can be energy-retaining and some serve as an energy conduit during the duration of your spell. The magickal instruments you use should connect naturally to the person you are using them with; they may be thought of as the extension of your body. as an example the wand can be described as an extension of the hand.

A few common tools for magickal use include:

Candles

Incense

Gemstones and crystals

Herbs

Knife or a wand

A cauldron

A crystal chalice

Tools that are optional

Personal tools

Candles

Candles have been extensively covered in the preceding chapter.

Incense

Incense is burned to deflect evil energies and also acts as a means for bringing us into peace or, in more intense instances it can induce in some cases, trance. The type of incense used will depend on the specific spell being used. But, if you're uncomfortable with the scent of one particular scent, you may substitute it with an alternative that you're drawn to.

Crystals and Gemstones

The applications of crystals as well as gemstones were covered in the previous chapters.

Herbs

Herbs were extensively discussed in the previous chapters.

Wand or Knife

An opener for letters A sword or a wand already made is a good option when a spell calls for this.

Cauldron

Useful for burning paper and to mix herb mixtures.

Chalice

When drinking is a essential ritual.

Optional Tools

Tarot cards, figurine, cross, pendulum, pentacle symbol.

Personified Tools

Items that are dear to you items that you are naturally drawn by This might be your most cherished necklace, or a ring given through your grandmother e.t.c.

Chapter 8: Spells

We will now explore how to cast spells correctly. Keep in mind that spells are templates designed to help the user. As you learn and get better at it and more proficient, you are able to modify the spells to fit your personal needs.

It is important to note that all spells must begin by making a drawing. The most common form for all spells is the circle.

Health Spells

Spells for health are a bit difficult and must be handled cautiously. There are both negative and positive health spells. Spells for negative health can result in devastating effects as they are by relying on the strength of your spiritual. This means that if the target has more strength than the one that casts the spell the spell will reverse and then harm the person casting the spell. If both are of the similar strength, the spell will be inactive until either of them becomes weak and it will begin to begin to take effect. Thus, health spells that are negative in nature are not recommended. Although health spells can be beneficial however, they're best utilized in conjunction with religious spells. As an example, a healing spell to treat the treatment of an illness could be done in conjunction with a protection spell for precautionary measures. We strongly advise against to apply this method to replace regular medical treatment provided by professional. This is intended to serve as a supplement to treatment.

Basic Moon Water Healing Spell

Tools

A glass of moon-water

Day

Every day that the waxing or full moon is on.

The moon's phase

Full moon, waxing moon.

How can you use the spell?

Put the glass with the moon's waters between your hands.

You can say exactly what you'd like moonwater to help you heal from.

Place the glass with your hands for around three minutes while you imagine the healing process.

Sip slowly the water immediately afterward.

Constant and Complete Wellbeing

Tools

A small bowl

Rainwater is an element that was charged during the storm by lightning or thunder.

Red, white and blue candle

Day

Every day during the week

Moon phase

Waxing moon

How can you use the spell?

1. Put the candles on a row on the floor in front of you. To the right is red, white in the middle blue towards the left.

2. Put your hands in the bowl of water, and put your hands on your chest. Say "The soundness of my human body belongs to me.'

3. Place your fingers in the water bowl and apply pressure to your forehead. Say "soundness of the your mind comes from mine.'

4. Place your finger in the water bowl and place it on forehead, affirming that your spirit is happy.'

5. Burn your candles.

6. It is important to flush the water out, preferring to pour it on a plant. Make sure to not store the rest of the water inside your house.

Anger Control Spell

Tools

Paper

A pen

Matches, lighters, or even matches

You can burn anything that you want to burn

Silver, black blue and black candle

Day

Every day of the week, excluding the Wednesdays and Thursdays.

The moon's phase

Waning moon or dark moon

How can you use the spell?

Place the candles in a line on the table in front of your. The left side is blue, the right side is black towards the center, and silver on the right.

Make sure to light the candles.

Make sure you write clearly, and don't hold your anger regarding in your paper. You can even include names in the event that you're angry with yourself Be expressive.

The paper should be burned in the cauldron or whatever vessel you prefer.

Once the paper has burned after the paper is burned, you can say:

"I take a decision now

I am about to start living to live, and I am happy,

My anger has been slashed the burden of my anger has been lifted. Blessings to you,

I'm rejuvenated, I'm free".

Career/Job Spell

A Three-Day Spell to Get a Job

Tools

The job description that describes what you'd like to accomplish, either in writing or by you, or cut from the newspaper.

Three blue candles set in an order

Day

Wednesday for three nights

The moon's phase

The full moon is now in its new phase.

How can you use the spell?

The first evening, flick the candle that is to your left.

1. Read the job description you wrote or read the newspaper advertisement in your head, then speak it out loud.

"This job is mine. it's mine

as it gets closer will be"

Blowing out the candle, and then leave the description of your job in front to the candles.

At night two you should ignite the first and second candles. Read the description of your job, and after which repeat the spell word as well as adding

"......so as close as I'm seeing, this job is going to very shortly be mine."

Blowing out both candles. Set the task information on the ground in front of the candles.

3. On the night of the third lighting the three candles, then read the text and repeat the words.

"This is my job; this is my job.

always closer and closer I am now able to see.

this job has now been given to me."

Allow the candle to flame, and go out to burn the paper, and declare:

"The job is easy and arrives at me."

4. On the fourth day, you can apply for the position or check on the application you have already completed.

Spell for Business Boom

Tools

Golden candle

A deep green candle

Patchouli and orange oils

Day

Sunday or Thursday

The moon's phase

Full moon and waxing moon

How do you perform the spell?

Start by lighting the dark green candle place the oil onto each candle, begin from the middle of the candle and then move it loosely towards the top, and finally down to the bottom.

Repeat the process for the golden candle.

The light in the dark green candle to the left side and place the gold candle to the right.

- Light both candles, and affirm

"as the dusk turns into dawn,

So will my company (mention"the name" of your company in this section) flourish and grow."

Allow the candles to be burned out.

Getting a Lucrative Job Spell

Tools

Gold pen

1 1/2 teaspoons of sage that has been dried

Silver candle

Holder for candles

A green piece of paper

Matches, lighters, or lighters

Three mint leaves

Day

Thursday

The moon's phase

Waxing moon, Full moon or waxing moon

How do you perform the spell?

On the green piece of paper, trace an etagram, with the point of the star facing upwards.

Write down the kind of job you're looking for in the middle of the pentagram. You could include the sum you'd like to earn as a pay as well.

Place the dried sage into the pentagram.

Cut the mint leaves into fragments and then place them inside the pentagram, too.

The candle should be placed in the holder, then place it over the mint and sage leaves.

The candle should be lit and you can tell the story:

"Goddess Morrigan, harken my plea,

Find me a task to assist my family members,

give me a job I'll love,

I am sending these phrases of prayer for the God of heaven".

The candle is supposed to burn over night until it is completely burned out, and then carefully take the paper close to the window (if you performed the spell within the room) and breathe to release the contents of your paper up into the air.

Prosperity Spell

Tool

The wallet of your

A brand new gold key that unlocks the door to nothing

Four candles of green

Day

Sunday, Wednesday and Wednesday, Sunday and Thursday

The moon's phase

The full moon, or the waxing moon

How can you use the spell?

Put the candles on the four points which are your North, South, East and West on the formation.

Make the word "prosperity" on the candle before you using the keys.

Lighting the candles.

Keep the key in your wallet, and tell it to:

"the earth", the wind sea, the sun

make it possible to use this fundamental crucial

My finances will prosper with the sun,

Health and wealth come out and are abounding".

Burn your candles.

Love Spells

Finding New Love

Tools

A favorite jewelry

The lavender or rose sticks inside a holder

A green candle

Day

Friday

Moon phase

Full moons, new moons full moon

How do you perform the spell?

You can cast your form.

The candle should be lit.

Place the necklace before the candle.

Concentrate your attention at the flame, and then say these phrases;

"I appeal to my loved ones to those who need me. Look for me, search me, and be by me faithfully, honestly and lovingly for until the day shines and the rivers flow across the earth."

The incense stick is lit by the candle. Write identical phrases in the air above the candle by using the stick to act for smoke pen.

Then, pass the jewellery over the candle, in an upward direction in a clockwise fashion three times and repeat the phrases.

Blowing out the candle, repeat the words.

The next time you're going to an appointment or a party in which you're hoping to meet somebody new, don't forget to wear the jewellery.

Victorian Mirror Spell

Tools

Mirrors that you are able to easily see yourself within

A hairbrush

Candles that smell of flowers

Day

Every day until midnight

Moon phase

The waxing moon and new moon full moon

How can you use the spell?

Roll your formation.

About two or three minutes before midnight, you should light the candle, and ensure the candle is placed so that it is reflected in the mirror.

When it is midnight, stand in front of the mirror, and begin to brush your hair with a gentle pace, while simultaneously, at the same time counting silently up to 100.

As you count down up to 100, say these three words, while brushing your hair.

"come my beloved", visit me across the mountains, oversea or over the rivers. Far or near to this looking

"The glass appears".

If you're in a state of trance let the brush go gently, then gently kiss the mirror, keeping your eyes shut.

Close your eyes slowly, blink. You might at any moment glimpse the picture of your love Don't be scared. You may recognize someone that whom you've already met or someone who you might be able to meet in the future.

*If you are unable to notice anything, close your eyes, count up until 100, then picture the reflection of the candle within your head. In the next moment, an image of your loved one would be visible.

Traditional Crescent Moon Spell to Attract New Love

Tools

Magnets

A box of pin

Maps of your town or even your country, if you're willing to have a friend of a different race.

Day

All night long from the time of waxing until the full moon

Moon phase

Waxing moon till full moon

How do you perform the spell?

Make your choice.

Place the pins on the map. Recite the following words:

"near and far" over ocean and land my true love, I would like to call you.

The magnet should be passed over the pins in a clockwise direction and then collect every pin.

Say continuously;

"so how do I make the love of my life, just as if I pin you to the magnet. Joined are we. Therefore, I declare my love real, and come before the next moon appears".

The map should be placed within the box, and then place it on top of the map.

Set the box next to the window.

If the moon's fullness is near when the moon is full, light a candle of silver to ensure that the light from the candle shines through the box along with the illumination from the moon.

Let everything be as it is until the moment you feel love. Repetition at each lunar new moon until you achieve the results you want.

Getting a Lover's Commitment

Tools

A ripe apple, or a different fruit you like in the event that they don't enjoy apple.

A silver knife

Day

At any time during the moon's waxing phase.

Moon phase

Waxing moon

How can you use the spell?

Clean the fruit with flowing water. Recite the following phrases:

"Fruit sweet" as the person takes a bite and changes (insert name) into a permanent state.

Sweet fruit sweet as one is eating, do not doubt

As my partner and I take in, do not delay to accept the offer,

Two of us"Our lives together for ever".

If the chance presents an opportunity, split the fruit into equal parts and share the fruit with your favorite person. When eating, the eater should recite these words to your brain three times.

Collect all remnants of your loved one's fruit and then bury them along with the ones you have, either on the ground or an empty pot. Recite the same words over and over.

Spirituality

Seeking Purpose

Tools

A candle of purple

A tiny piece of amethyst

A tiny crystal of clear quartz

Drawstring bags or anything which can be used to hold them as a garment.

Day

Monday, Sunday or on Thursday

The moon's phase

Full moon, waxing moon, or waxing moon

How do you perform the spell?

The stones should be placed in the bag or on the cloth, and say

"These stones I hold are also conductors.

with visions and answers which will be revealed

In my dreams in my dreams, I'll see in my dreams what I know to be real

My destiny will be made clear".

Lay the stones in a bag beneath your pillow.

Attention to your desires for 3 days, and watch for any signs or clues.

Receiving Divine Messages

To perform this spell, you must have an understanding of how to read Tarot cards, and practicing. Be patient by the fact that you can't do it right the first time.

Tools

Tarot cards

Two candles of purple as well as two candles in yellow

Day

Monday, Sunday, or Thursday, or Thursday, Friday or Sunday

Moon phase

Full moon and waxing moon

How do you perform the spell?

Put the candles on a row with this arrangement: one candle in purple before your face and one on your left. The yellow candle should be to your left while the other one is to the right.

Make the candles light and then say;

"a look through this channel will bring forth

Bright may be it and true to the sun rises

and visions of dancers on the night

My message is visible".

Get three tarot cards and interpret them in the same way.

Another alternative is to say;

"a look through this channel reveals

Bright may be it and true to the daybreak

With visions of dancing at the night

the message I'm sending is visible

when the next full moon comes around I dreamed that night at the next full moon, my messages will I get".

Write the date for the full moon to come on your calendar. Pay close attention to any your dreams are.

Fathering

Tools

Candles in pink

Lilac and rose incense

Day

Monday, Sunday, Friday or the Saturday

Moon phase

Full moon and waxing moon

How can you use the spell?

1. The candle is lit and placed in the front of you.

2. The incense should be burned.

3. Shut your eyes and concentrate on the thing you desire for approximately one minute.

4. Following that, you should recite the following sentences:

"A father I am as it is.

The understanding that love comes from me

can the universe for my child show

my heart the love I have, the way I experience".

5. When you have finished the poem, close your eyes once more and keep focusing on the happy moments with your children.

Fertility and Childbirth

To Increase Preconception Energy

Tools

Small white flowers

Silver-colored dish, half-filled with water

Silver candles (if done indoors)

Day

Every day before you attempt to conceive the birth of a child.

Moon phase

Waxing up to the complete moonstone

How can you use the spell?

Take a walk under the moon with your back to it. If inside, you can light the candles of silver close to an unclosed window so that the moon's light can shine through.

Set the bowl that contains water so that the moon's or candle will shine

Set the flowers in the water and say

"lady moon, I'm calling your fertility in this water

That you allow me to have an offspring that is healthy

Bright as your light soft as the glow of your eyes,

to be able to discern when the time is to be, and also the pleasures of pregnancy and conception"'.

The bowl should be covered by a mesh cover to prevent dirt from entering.

At the beginning of the day, strain the water, then refrigerate.

Each day and at evening, rub some of the water onto your womb. Repeat the phrases.

Repeat this process until conception.

To Conceive a Child

If you are able, go through this routine with a partner.

Tools

A scarf in pink

A pink rose quartz crystal, a pearl or, a pink glass bead

Long silver pins, large needle or, a the thin knife made of paper

Day

Three nights preceding the full moon.

Moon phase

Waxing up to the full moon

How can you use the spell?

The first night take the crystal and place it on the hand that you don't write on and place the pins to the hand you write on.

Place the hands in a row making sure they aren't touching. Repeat these phrases;

"so do two be three. baby"we as we welcome you into our family." families."

Put them out on the windows in your bedroom and do exactly the same thing for the next and third night.

At night, when there is a full moon, gently touch to the crystal using the sharp end of the pin, and repeat those words once more.

Love your lover.

Next day you wrap the crystal with the pink scarf and put it in the drawer of your bedroom until you are able to think of it.

Miscellaneous Spells

A Two-Day Safety on A Journey Spell

Tools

A talisman

Water element

A Chalice

Silver candle, a red, brown, and a white candle

Lavender incense

Day

Every day during the week

Moon phase

New moon or waxing moon

How can you use the spell?

The day before Set the brown, silver and red candles on the table in a line. The red candle is to the right with brown on the middle and silver on the left then, ignite the candles.

Incense is burned.

Put the talisman into the bowl.

Completely cover the talisman by the element water.

Put your palms on the water. Close enough but not touching, and affirm:

"elements that create this water

This charm is a charge, and I ask to thee

With the power to keep and guard".

Repeat the process three times.

Burn candles and place the talisman in a place where it is lit by the moon and sun could be charged for all day (the sun must be shining brightly in order to charge your talisman). If you are experiencing cloudy weather, keep it in place until the sun has risen and it is recharged.

Once the talisman has been fully charged, you can put it back into the water, and then place it on your desk.

Light the candle, and then put the candle in front of you and then repeat:

"the mother moon as well as the father sun have given this piece a blessing

My safety is assured my safety is assured, and all worries are gone

This amulet is solid and crystal transparent.

I'm able to travel with confidence through the entire all the time of the".

Carry your talisman wherever you need to.

Chapter 9: What Is Wicca?

Wicca is a popular 20th-century cult of contemporary witchcraft, which helps its followers develop an increased connection to Nature as well as Mother Earth. With its rituals and teachings that are based on the religion of Wicca encourages awareness, love and reverence towards nature, the Sun and the sun moon, the Moon, rivers, wind, rain and mountains and the animal kingdom. blossoms and plants, earth beneath our feet, and the beautiful autumn colors and winter snow.

Wicca shows us that all around us is composed out of energy and is a belief in the dual nature within all things. This implies the existence of the concept of God and Goddess. They are the feminine and masculine energies as well as the negative and positive. The entire Universe is made up of this energies and Nature itself is an amazing expression of the principle of duality humans are able to hold the flame of duality within us.

In Wicca The Gods and Goddesses exist present within us and in us. They are depicted as gentle and loving entities The gods are not violent to their kids, they don't hold grudges, they do not are not averse to punishment and don't create Heaven or Hell. They are instead kind, compassionate and advocate for respect and fairness.

Wicca is a way to take complete responsibility for the actions we take and doesn't support any behaviour or claims made by any external force, like the Devil who manipulates us to do things that are not good.

That's where the concept of Karma takes place and it is believed that whatever you give to the world returns to you through energy, people, or the circumstances. Wiccans don't believe the existence of Satan as well as any other symbol of Evil. These concepts are typically found in Christian doctrines. Additionally, there isn't any claims of absolute particularity regarding this being the only way towards peace, knowledge or wisdom. The teachings of Wicca allow the person to discover and select the path that best suits them through the world. The Wiccan philosophy is founded on the idea in the fact that Nature is sacred and Life should be treated with respect no matter its form in the medium through which it manifests.

Wiccan Spells

Wiccan spells are usually categorized in two distinct types, "White magic" being associated with respectable and high points, and "Dark Magic" frequently associated with hateful of evil deeds.

A lot of advanced Wiccans are now avoiding the duality and claim that the dark shading is just another shade which has been created by Hollywood as well as the actual shade itself should not be associated to sinister ritual or hate regardless of imagination.

Wiccans believe that magic spell casting is an essential natural law. This is a principle that even we cannot seem to comprehend. The various followers of the Wicca Religion do not claim that they understand how their magical system operates in any way by imagination. However, it is enough that it seems to function and that they've observed it in action for themselves.

The majority of Wiccans describe Wiccan magic and Wiccan Magic as "the Art of bringing about changes according to one's personal Will." The word Wiccan is essentially a reference to any person who adheres to Wiccan practices. Wiccan Religion.

The Wiccan spell can be described as a the practice of ritual or training that results in quantifiable changes to the body or in the enthusiastic circle, as a result of the intentions of at minimum one Wiccans that are casting the spell.

Wiccan spells that are typically practiced contain love spells, mending spells, ripeness and other spells. These are used for the purpose of helping to get rid of the worst effects.

The Wiccan Sacred Circle

Wiccans frequently cast spells in rituals in the develop known as "the Sacred Circle," seeking to bring about changes in their lives.

The term "Sacred Circle" refers to Sacred Circle can be described as a circular or a circle that is and blessed by Wiccans for either to hold vitality and form a sacred area or form a barrier to safety. A Sacred Circle can sometimes be the latter.

sacred Circles can be made by creating an elongated ring of chalk or salt. Some Wiccans may even mark lines in the earth every now and then it could be thought of by Wiccans. Wiccan Witch to produce the same results. Similar round-ups are seen in a few Eastern religious systems.

Wiccan spells, on the majority of cases they are used to achieve a positive outcome for the community. However, the reality is that most spells being cast by Wiccans (just as the many other followers and adherents from these "Old Religious Traditions") are cast to help achieve positive purposes and not for malicious reasons.

The Law of Threefold Return

It is evident in this in the Wiccan Rede that declares "it is not hurt anyone, just do whatever you want." A lot of Wiccans also believe in an additional aspect of Wiccan ethics, that can be described as "The Law of Threefold Return."

The law states that if you pay no attention to the type of Wiccan spell is used whether it is big-hearted or shady, the results that are triggered by the spell return to the person who cast it with a triple the strength or power.

It is identical to the Eastern way of thinking about Karma which was first adopted after a long time but later appearing throughout different forms in the Buddhist, Jain, Sikh and Hindu ways of thinking. One reason is the reason Wicca is often referred to as the spiritual practice that is a part of western culture.

Yoga as a whole an integral part of all six school of the Hindu approach to thinking. It is all about controlling and prepping for the mind to attain a state with a profound and unsurpassed knowledge as well as tranquility. Many advanced Wiccans consider this message as having a rational meaning to their beliefs too.

Wiccan Spells can be found in many forms and styles as the practice of casting spells in a respectful and gentle attitude, you'll be amazed by the sheer number of traditional natural religions. For instance, Wicca can be fulfilling and fulfilling the same amount of increasingly traditional and modern beliefs.

Instructions to Create Your Wiccan Spells

Digging Into Witchcraft

If you come across spells you've come to be quite enthralling However, you'd be more confident regarding them if you were able to "change" some aspects, then you could use spells that are available in books or available on the internet. When you alter the spells according to your preferences There are some points to be considered. In the first place, remember that when you adapt spells that are based on other books, these adjustments are intended for use to the extent that it is. Many agnostic writers have spells that can be adjusted However, you want to avoid infringing upon the copyright rights of authors or online academics in sharing the altered work either on the internet or off with the permission from the original authors of the altered work.

Before writing or modifying spells using any method, make sure you take a look at what you really need "watch what you desire" can be interpreted here. Be sure to know the things you require, but what you are looking for, and the way you expect the desires you have will manifest. Also, you should be aware of any possibilities that may arise from your actions. Sometimes when working on magick you may end in a situation that is exactly what you want, however it's not what you expected. That is the reason why precision is crucial to the process.

No matter if you're altering spells that you've turned out to be a bit shrewd or writing your own spells with prior preparation, you'll need keep the goal in at the bottom of your brain. Every word you use in your spell should be aligned with your goals and expected result. In this regard being precise when casting your spells will be the determining factor in the success of the spell casting attempts. For the purpose of ensuring that you are specific of your writing You can finish the language and timing of your work. Additionally, it is possible to use magical correspondences.

Timing Certain practitioners time when a spell has been operating during a particular moon phase. In this case, it is possible to time spells when you are in the full, waxing or melting down moon stage. The moon's waxing phase is associated to beginnings, and it is associated with endings, and the slowing of the moon has a connection to endings. The full moon is associated with the entire magickal process. If you're directing the spell that you want the event to be over then you could time your actions to coincide with the moment when the winding moon is visible, and when you're looking for a new starting point in your situation when the moon is waxing, it's the ideal time to carry out the work. Some practitioners also time their work based on dates of the week, seasons, the planetary time, or the strange correspondences.

Rhymes Not all words rhyme, however you might discover that you're more receptive to work with rhyme. It will be easier to remember, and using rhymes, you create an impression through your words to anyone who can hear. When you create your personal spells, it is important take the time to remember the words you've written. This way take your time giving full attention to the words you're using rather than merely interpreting them on a piece of paper.

Perception The spell you choose to use needs be precise and exact in its wording. It will not only help you to communicate your desires verbally however, you'll also require words that activate your visualization abilities. The more clearly you visualize your dream and the greater your chances of achieving your desired outcome. Before you begin working on to cast a spell, it's wise idea to invest some time in imagining the outcome you want to achieve. As with the spell's description, when you imagine your desired outcome, be as precise as you can be possible, and visualize the desired result in every possible aspect.

If you're the type of Witch who is practicing the Wiccan religion, you'll have be sure that the casting's language and desired outcome aligns to the Wiccan Rede of "hurt no one, and do as you want." If you're an Wiccan practitioner, you need be concerned about being aware of the Threefold Law of Return and the possibility of a kickback in the form of a demonstration that carries negative energy. Make sure that your spells work certain that the energy you receive when you manifest will be positive.

How do you become a wiccan?

1. Peruse

If you are considering switching into Wicca prior to deciding whether or not you want to make any decisions or beliefs, it is advisable take some time to think about it. We're sorry to inform you, but if you're not interested in perusing or contemplating, then you're likely to dislike Wicca in the least Or perhaps you're likely to be getting little out of it. Wicca is not a dogmatic religion instead of revealing the truth about what it believes and what it believes, it throws the ball around and encourages you to consider in a fundamental way. It requires knowledge.

A single book won't suffice but 5 or 10 books are an adequate starting point. It's by and large prescribed you read and study--effectively--for in any event a year and a day before settling on any choices about whether to be Wiccan or not.

Step 2: Think

Once you've started to figure more what you can about Wicca and its principles, beliefs and other such. It's time to consider whether your beliefs compatible. Do your beliefs fit into a system which could be a part of a Wiccan framework?

Wicca is definitely not the only religion that is dogmatic, which is a fact and therefore, anyone coming to it looking for an edict of a holy book or an overview of costs is attempting to approach this from a wrong angle. It is, in any event, Wicca is additionally not an untruthful, but as other sources generally have put the term, "anything you need it to be." The problem when you say Wicca is something is that it's saying something that's not. There are certain aspects that don't fall perfectly within the terms.

In other words, if you're not a believer in the existence of Gods or gods, but are looking to experience enchantment is it really a reason why you a part of a religion which the main practices, ceremonies, customs like these have a focus upon Pagan Gods and Goddesses? There is no reason not to study Witchcraft without becoming Wiccan at all. However in the event that you place your faith in Jesus in all your actions as a hero should you worship Jesus in a religion which says there's nothing that is exempt from being a part of?

The great thing about Wicca is the fact that there are any rules--there is no need to acknowledge that this is true or clarify methods of reasoning. Whatever the case may be, the context of a religious tradition that is experiential it is a requirement to use reason and logic, which is a means of evaluating whether your beliefs are compatible with Wicca or there are factors that draw your to Wicca could be located in a different religion that corresponds to your convictions.

Step 3: Pray

If you get to the core of the issue where you realise that you must be adored as the Wiccan Then it's time to reverse the process. Get yourself in touch with your Gods. Begin to connect with them with them, and then ask them to reveal their own self to you. ask for direction, clarification to understand.

Get started ruminating -because as is often stated, if you are communicating with God and reflection, you are tuning into. A daily reflection routine can benefit you for wellness and health goals, however it is not a good way to achieve spiritual development.

Step 4: Observe

Begin to monitor the world through an Wiccan view. Follow the cycles of seasons, as well as the cycle that the moon makes. Begin to recognize them in small ways. Take into consideration Wiccan principles and morals whenever you're faced with making choices. Take a look at your own life as well as the areas where exercises could be benefited from Wicca.

Pay attention to your environment; you can observe the interaction between each living creature. Be aware of the cycles of the cycles of the seasons, moon, and of the world. Perhaps you'd like to incorporate these cycles involved in a more regular daily routine with reflections and prayers or begin some simple, informal practices to keep Esbats as well as Sabbats.

The process of studying and reading should never stop. However, it's crucial to start making use of these rules. This is the way to begin being a part of Wicca.

Step 5: Build

The most common mistake people do right from the start is rushing out in a rush to collect equipment. However, Wicca isn't a scrounger to. However, in the meantime after you've begun to begin to practice, it might be time move towards more regular exercises. It is possible to start making use of special tools to raise your area. However, you do not need these at the exact time. It is a good idea to look at a tool's capabilities for its function, then after which, you can look for it and start using it, taking it one at a time.

A lot of books can help users to purchase various items However, keep in mind that you don't require every instrument that a book discusses. That's why it's crucial to know the capacity of tools before even thinking about buying it. You might wind in something that you don't need to be concerned about.

Additionally, it's time to begin constructing your own ritual. This means creating a more organized method to manage your ceremony. It's not necessary to plan every detail for your ritual, but by the very definition of a ritual the term "ritual" refers to an old-fashioned practice. It is a way to attain a sense of ritual. This assists you in escaping the stage of awareness in which you're actually thinking in this state of mind where you are in autopilot in order of allowing yourself to different energies that you're trying to bring.

Consider a basic opening and closing the door, summoning, or making circles. It's also not necessary to perform all night long. Every couple of months, you should consider adding another element.

Step 6: Magic

It's not the main focus of Wicca. But it is an important part. At the end of the day, you'll need to incorporate some of them to your rituals. Anyone who is interested in studying enchantment does not have to be Wiccan and should go straight to studying The Craft; however, should Wicca as a religious practice is something that interests you, put in the effort of to get familiar with the faith prior to that. If you get close to the core of the issue, when you're gathering the tools and executing routine rituals, it's the suitable time to start practicing this fascinating and intriguing aspect. Include a couple of minor spooky roles in your hover to begin examining the manifestations of human behavior.

Step 7: Network

In the near future, it will be important to be involved in the Pagan community and get out in the wild. It's not necessary to wait till the finalization of this to make it happen but if you're not been there yet, then you must try now.

Begin to meet with other Wiccans attend workshops or open rituals, or Drumming circles. It can lead you up to new perspectives as well as help you meet people who are like you You may also discover some covens is something you'd like to be part of If this is your primary purpose. Religions can be considered as close-to-home adventure, however they're also a part of the world, and they're designed to be experienced with others in public.

This list in no shape, form or manner the most effective way of the process of becoming Wiccan but it may help if you're not sure how to start or where to start, this can be an acceptable way to help you get started.

Wiccan rituals

No matter if the occasion is Sabbat or an Esbat or a celebration such as an event that involves a handfasting (wedding) or a ceremony of start, or an element of an arrangement covens and members of the circle are gathered to share their love to honor the Goddess as well as God and praise the amazing things to be discovered throughout the cycle of the world. Although the majority of Wiccan ceremonies are conducted privately, a handful of covens do perform their rituals to the public to ensure that everyone who wishes to attend can learn about the Craft. A lot of Wiccan communities do this or even invite everyone to participate.

The solo rituals are equally important, and solo Wiccans recognize this when they believe in their religion at all times on the Wheel of the Year, they contribute their energy and energy to the larger group. the supernatural power of these amazing rituals.

RUDIMENTS OF WICCAN RITUALS

Rich, beautiful, bizarre and encouraging Wiccan rituals are able to take on various forms that are unique, with no two rituals identical. Certain rituals are extremely organized and elaborate. It's the norm when it comes to coven rituals. but since the majority of covens maintain the nuances of their rituals hidden, only to those who are not yet initiated, it is difficult to describe these with a lot of detail. The various rituals, specifically ones performed by single or diverse Wiccans could be truly simple by association or could be created in the moment.

The essence of a random Wiccan ceremony will depend on the particular event. As an example, Esbats which are also known as Full Moon festivities, are solely focused on the

Goddess and Sabbats are a celebration of the shared connection of God and Goddess. God. Of all possible variations regardless of what they can, there's two essential aspects that can, generally will be integrated in what is referred to as the "common" ceremony.

At the start the purification process begins that includes both the celebrant(s) as well as the location where the event is being held. It could be an ritual shower or even a smearing ceremony to remove any unwelcome forces from the area of the ritual regardless of whether it's outside the home or within the house. Smearing involves the consumption of sacred herbs such as rosemary, sage along with lavender.

The process of setting up an altar is immediately. Some Wiccans have an altar for the duration of time at their residences, but in this case, the altar will change depending on the occasion, such as getting fall leaves for Mabon (the Autumn Equinox) or Samhain (otherwise known as Halloween.) The altar is set up using the various Wiccan tools, images and other contributions spread according to different rituals.

Following is the ritual of throwing the circle. It is a way of demonstrating which creates a boundary between sacred space as well as the everyday, normal world. The altar usually is located at the centre of the circle. It has plenty of room for the people who must work freely within the circle and without the risk of straying out of the boundaries. The circle could be divided by the sea salt of a lengthy line, some stones, plants or even candles. There are many ways to perform throwing a circle, and you are able to look over in depth on this page.

If the circle is cast at the beginning of the ceremony, it begins to call for. It is possible to change the order However, generally God as well as the Goddesses are welcomed to be part of the celebration following which the four elements--Earth Air, Fire and Water are summoned as they're the primary elements in the midst of the existence. (In many rituals, the fifth element--Akasha (or Spirit) is also included.) Different traditions use this is referred to by the name of Calling the Quarters, and the four bearers (North, East, South as well as West) are considered to be regardless of or instead of the Elements.

After these actions have been completed then the heart of the ceremony begins. To begin with, the aim of the event is expressed-- regardless of whether it's to commend a Sabbat or an Esbat, or maybe to request of the God and Goddess for the benefit of somebody who needs mending or some other sort of help. (Enchanted work of magic can serve as the focal point of rituals. But, many Wiccans perform this ritual separately apart from Sabbat rituals to preserve the emphasis on goddesses and God on Sabbats.)

Once the purpose is stated then the primary part of the ceremony could consist various activities. A point of convergence may consist of the presenting of a show that is ritualistic such as acting out scenes from antiquated stories or ballads, as well as other ritualistic materials depending on the custom of Wicca that the group is adhering to. Single Wiccans might also peruse old messages from other worlds and even write their unique verses for the occasion. Moving, singing, or reciting along with other ritual movements could be part of the procedure, and so could simply thinking of the blessings of the festive season. The possibility of offering petitions is there in any way, whether they're personal or to purposes of helping others. In certain religions, it is essential that ritual spaces are used in order to aid the entire community or everyone.

A ritual called "cakes and beers" (or "cakes along with wines") is a key part of Wiccan ceremonies. The offering of drink and food is made as symbols of blessing to God or Goddess. It is usually in connection with the ceremony's arrangement (albeit certain traditions begin by offering the word "cakes and beer"). The purpose of this ritual is to connect the spiritual and Earth plane, as well as to help ground and focuses the participants prior to ending the rituals. It is a great time to be a part of the ritual, Elements and the Goddess as well as God are publicly expressed their gratitude to and released from while the circle is closed.

This is the only format is what a Wiccan ritual will typically follow. If you're a member of a set coven or a circle it most likely will come up with its own interpretation of the one above and there are many possible variations. If you're an individual expert and want to learn more about the specific traditions you want to follow as well as create your own unique Wiccan rituals. In any time the goal is sincere and you're focused on what you are doing, there is any way you can do this "wrong"!

Nearly every religion integrates sacred objects to its worship and ritual. No matter if it's the rarest ceremonial vestments, religious costumes or statues of gods revered in sanctuaries, candles the talismans, chalices and other symbols, people are creating and using tangible objects -also known as "tools"for centuries to maintain their spiritual focus and energy in the rituals they engage in.

Wicca is the practice of using some tools, each one has a symbolic significance, a specific use and a particular place in the Wiccan altar in a ritual.

A "HANDS-ON" PHILOSOPHY

Wiccan ritual instruments are used to direct and focus energy that is spiritual (or "mystic") power to allow for communication properly with the highest. It is a subtle, yet important difference, however there is a distinction between this ritual as well as the use of symbolic objects in various faiths. Wiccans recognize that they participate with the creative powers of nature as illustrated by goddess as well as God and are not submissive to the desires of an apex power.

In this way, the instruments that are used in Wiccan rituals are both symbolic as well as practical, because each item and every action performed within the sacred circle is designed to challenge and harness this creative power. Instruments are employed to summon and invoke divinities as well as energies of the Elements as well as to carry out rituals of a mystical nature, and protect against negative energetic impact, in addition to other capacities. However, it is important to recognize that instruments don't possess supernatural power on their own. Instead, they are merely a way to enhance personal power for the Wiccan using the tools.

"THE LIST" OF WICCAN TOOLS

The specific arrangement of the instruments used in rituals that are considered to be essential to Wiccan practices will vary based on the particular tradition. Some covens and solitaries are known to greatly expand rituals by using an assortment of items, while other remain largely simple using a handful of tools to perform various functions. In the end, the most frequently referred to instruments that are used for a crucial ritual is the Chalice (or cup) and the wand. the pentacle, athame (or ritual knife), that is articulated as "a-that-may") and the censer (for incense) as well as at least one candle.

As well as other instruments that are referred to as referenced and, in this case could be considered fundamental tools, based on the tradition of the cauldron, the broom and the ringer, as well as the sword, the staff as well as the ritual scourge. In addition, there are many things that are part of ritual, but aren't considered "tools" on their own like images of God as well as the Goddess and boline (an extremely sharp knife that is used to cut and slice) as well as a platter to serve food for the ritual and other items, such as valuable stones and plants, ornaments and altar material as well as other items.

It's not to the least necessity to keep the tools you need for the first time to practice Wicca. It's generally recommended that you start small. Get tools every couple of turns, and gradually build your rituals while you progress.

STARTING POINTS OF RITUAL PRACTICE

If you are a newcomer to Wicca These tools might appear in some ways unorthodox and arbitrary. Are things such as knives, cups, ringers and pentacles considered essential to connect with the soul? There are many possible responses to this question, but to the point that at the end day, it takes some effort time, effort, and patience to the instruments of ritual that can make "sense" for an experienced. This is an important part of the motive to read for the duration of a whole year, and one day before taking on practicing Wicca. Furthermore, it reveals the most you can about the background of its development, and the many religious traditions it takes its inspiration from, many are rooted in the ancient relic.

Chapter 10: World Of Wicca

The thing that many across the globe don't know is the fact that Wicca is actually a religious practice, often referred to as 'Benevolent Witchcraft "The Old Religion" and also 'The Craft'. This old craft is element of our modern pagan religion, also known as natural spirituality.

Paganism is the name given to people who adhere to a faith or practice that isn't Christianity, Judaism, Buddhism or Hinduism. It is a religion that includes Wiccans. Wiccan faith is part of Paganism together with Pantheists, Heathens, Goddess Spirituality folk Ecofeminist, Unitarian Universalist Pagans, Animists, Druids, ChristoPagans as well as any other Nature connected spirituality practices.

However, within these religions there is a range of communities, each with a distinct goals, beliefs dimensions, sizes, orientation symbols, and structure. There are several different kinds of rituals within the Wiccan religion. These include Shamanic, Alexandrian, British Traditionalist, Gardnerian, Faerie Traditions of the family, Hereditary, Celtic, Circle Crat, Dianic, Eclectic Craft as well as many more paths and cultural practices.

Some of these groups also have different practice and group. Certain Wiccan religions are initiated however there are some that aren't. A lot of the practices that initiate differ from other traditions and some of them offer initiations through spiritual aids and groups, instructors, as well as gods in dreams or visions and as well as quests.

There are many differities among a wide range of people and religions, yet they all share a love for Nature. People seek harmony and peace with each other and the environment around them. A lot of practitioners can connect and befriend numerous animals, plants, and spirits who live on the Earth alongside us. They also honor naturally occurring cycles in nature for example, the new moon as well as when the full moon is in. There are many who enjoy rituals at these times by harnessing the energies of earth's element. People who adhere to the Wiccan belief system are often referred to as "witches".

In the Wiccan religion, as well as in other Paganism faiths, there's an idea that each human or animal, stream or rock, tree and various other types of nature have a divine spirit inside. In several traditions, aside from the Paganism religion, they possess an orthodox monotheistic aspect in which they worship only one divine God to whom they believe. In Paganism as well as other religions they also have an element of polytheism where there is various Divine manifestations like Gods, Goddesses, as well as numerous other forces of the spiritual. The universe and nature have a significant role to play in the manner the Wiccan beliefs are shaped.

Chapter 11: The Energy Of The Moon

The energies of the sun and the moon have played a role in shaping the course of our development throughout the course of our lives, and also. Humans, along with any other living thing in the earth, are all in an intense connection with the energy of our celestial bodies. This is especially true for the moon. It is the source of many of the experiences and emotions which we often call our "intuition" and that is the reason that many believe that women are more naturally intuitive than males as they possess a greater connection to feminine energy that emanate from the moon, which results in a higher degree of ability to sense than men.

The sensitivity we feel to the energy of the sun and moon are commonly referred to by the term "sixth sense" it is one of the greatest instruments we can are able to use when performing the art of magic. However, it is especially relevant to moon magic.

If we're practicing moon magic among the ways we usually start with is by making an "appeal" towards the moon, and then form an interconnection with it for time during the ritual, however, the connection made isn't necessarily true. it is actually that the relationship exists between us and the moon grows stronger as we allow ourselves to the lunar energy and permit the channel created by the energy of this moon to expand in its size.

If this happens during the conjunction of the moon particularly during the times of the full moon as well as the new moon, which is when it is most powerful the connection can allow us to increase the strength of magic spells as well as other types of magic that we do.

It is crucial to realize that various phases of the moon create slightly different energies which are suitable in different ways or different types of magicks.

Every one of the phases of the moon has the energy of different kinds and can be used in different forms of magic as well as to achieve different purposes.

Our connection to the moon and the magical acts we do through the energy it gives us seems to change in accordance with the various moon phases.

While the moon waxes and its energy increases, it will be at its maximum and it is able to better utilize the purpose of magic to boost energy or potential and energy, whereas the magic performed at the end of the lunar cycle most effective to perform magic intended to reduce the force of energy or potential for example, to cleanse or eliminate undesirable energy.

The middle of the lunar cycle is commonly known as harvest. It it is the time to commemorate the achievements achieved and the rewards which have been harvested from early in the lunar cycle. It is similar to the harvest was named after it.

The second part of lunar cycles used to clean up after the fact, and then releasing the energy and all the things that don't need attention no longer.

In the New Moon when new goals are established for the new cycle that can manifest similarly but then discarded as we enter the next cycle.

The lunar cycle is the progression of time that follows a steady course of events which allow the creation of things which will then be removed so that more creation of new items through an unending process of renewal.

Also, there are a few basics you can further enhance the magical job you do in the various phases of the lunar cycle. moon. The first phase of the lunar cycle is called the new moon. At the beginning of the new moon, the energy received from the moon is especially beneficial to setting goals for the remainder of the month, or to think about what could be built. Beginning new projects or tasks are more efficient at this point in the moon's cycle. anything is based on the attraction of particular energies will work well in the period.

The next phase, where the moon is rising to its highest level in the full moon and is known as"the waxing moon. It is the most beneficial period of the lunar cycle to harness the energy that we get from the moon to aid us move forward towards our goals we've decided to achieve. The next step following the start of new initiatives, so that we can advance and begin to take action so that we can achieve the objectives.

The positive energy you get in this stage is particularly beneficial in helping us achieve the objectives we might be working towards, and could prove extremely effective when it's applied to the work which is linked to the growth of types of energy. A few common instances are for creating or strengthening bonds between individuals, and enhancing physical or mental wellbeing.

The opposite of the waxing moon phase is called the waving moon. The waning moon phase occurs immediately following the full moon, and is ahead of it gets the moon's new phase. The energies you get during the full moon phase will be most beneficial for those who are seeking to counteract the energies of the moon that is waxing.

The rituals you do by utilizing the power of the moon's waning phase will work best for tasks such as releasing energy to get over obstacles that are in your way or to cleanse yourself from negative energies.

The lunar phase cycle often thought to be being the one with the strongest power can be described as the Full Moon. A lot of people believe that the full moon is the most significant and magical night of the lunar calendar, and they will seek to utilize the power of the full moon to create magic spells that are particularly important. This is why there are myths about werewolves and vampires and a myriad different supernatural creatures as well as events that occur during the night of the full moon.

The moon's power and the moon is at its highest and are greater than other phases of moon's cycle.

The lunar cycles are initiated with the moon's new phase. In this time the sun and moon are in perfect alignment, however the sun's reflection reflects away from Earth so that's the reason why we aren't able to be able to see the moon's glowing.

In these time the moon can rise and set in the course of the day. It is often impossible to observe the moon without the aid of a telescope. The new moon and the beginning of a new moon are basically similar to each other.

In these moments when you are stressed, it is essential to keep your focus on the goals you wish to see manifest within your life, such as goals and new projects.

Harnessing the New Moon's Energy. The ability to think clearly is the most important thing to this. The more you think, the better your energy flows. The trick is to be aware to the energy that you're using and what you wish to bring into your life. If you're conscious about your thought processes and you are able to control your thoughts and energies whatever you wish to achieve can be achieved.

Create a Vision Board. Your goal is to make the desires concrete. Things you can feel see, feel and make real.

It can be made using posters, magazines clippings glue, or even a poster board. Or you could go digital and create an image that you can share on Pinterest. The goal is to organize your thoughts all in one spot.

Once you've finished your list, examine every item, and think of what steps you'll need in order to make it take place. Do you think this will require an enormous amount of time? Do you have to ask for assistance from someone else? What are you required to accomplish to move things along?

You can find inspiration by setting out the steps for each goal. Inspiring people will help build momentum. the momentum will bring results.

Make a Sigil and Burn It. The sigils can be a wonderful opportunity to express your creativity while putting your energy, intentions and enthusiasm into the work you do.

First thing to do is gather some pieces of paper, and begin writing your thoughts about what you would like to come true throughout the moon's phase.

Once you've got your message Take it the way it was written then think of all the potential outcomes. The statement could be: "I would like to be a wealthy person."

This is fine, But what about the quantity of? Do you desire to have a lot of negative energy? Are you looking to achieve lots of weight? It is important to be specific. If you could say: "I want to live an active, healthy and happy lifestyle filled with abundant love".

This makes a lot more sense than you think, isn't it? After you have sent these messages out to the Universe it is impossible to have any confusion as to the fire you're setting to. Make sure to avoid the use of a different definition, if you can. Once you've got your goal, it's time to write it over again with no spaces. Also, remove all vowels as well as any characters that repeat. The result would be something similar to:

"wntlvhypfbd"

This can be a little hard to understand, doesn't it? At this point you can begin to blend the two words into an image. Put the arms and legs where they should not be and let your creativity flow. There's no wrong symbol. When you're done, by the time you're done your test, it ought to feel good. If it isn't, you can start again and continue until it feels right.

If you've found it, it's something that took the time, love as well as your attention and time. It has taken both sides of your brain to achieve this goal. The first 3 days in the cycle of the moon to harness moon's energies You must burn the moon's energy to let your strength and desires to the Universe for manifestation.

Momentum and the Waxing Moon. There are three phases to the waxing moon, and all are concerned the preparation to fulfill and accept your goals for the future.

The waxing Gibbous Moon: During this time it is important be able to redefine your goals and become more in tune to the current conditions. Utilize what's happened over these past weeks to determine what you have to work on to improve your goals. The direction you are heading for should be more clear now that you've taken steps to gain insight into your objectives and the way they're moving towards being achieved.

1. First Quarter Moon It's the ideal time to act. Determine the actions you must take to accomplish your goals. Do not get distracted whenever a problem arises. It is imperative to keep moving forward at this time.

Waxing Crescent Moon The time of waxing is the Waxing Crescent Moon. time you must think about and organize your goals. Share your hopes, desires and expectations out to the world. You should also consider the ways in which these issues are likely impact your daily life.

Harvest Time. Everything is already set to go into motion by this and the other new moons. It is the perfect time and is ready for you to cash on all the gifts you have received. Take a look at the present just in front of your face.

Are there any opportunities that have presented themselves to you which you may not have spotted? Do you sense a push driving you to take a new direction?

It is essential to remain vigilant attentive, alert, and open. You must listen to your whole heart to listen to what the moon's words tell you. Moon has power, knowledge, and wisdom to change your life.

Harnessing the Full Moon's Energy. Moon's energy is the highest when she's fully. It is a great time to focus on the full moon.

It is beneficial to charge your body in the full moon. Take a walk and enjoy the moon's beautiful light by embracing your spirit as well as your mind and heart.

It's the time to take advantage of positive possibilities when you are able you can make use of it effectively. You could boost your energy levels, but it can cause havoc to your mood.

As the full moon brings lots of energy, it is important to ensure that your thoughts are calm in order to reap the positive benefits. Be aware that what happens to your mind, spirit or body will get amplified dramatically.

If you're upset, you're going to be more angry. If you are feeling happy and content, you'll experience a greater sense of happiness.

If the moon is fully filled, the sea is likely to expand and emergency rooms always have many more patients. Her energy is powerful and you must direct your energy with positive thoughts.

Energy and enthusiasm are all going to increase. It will be a wonderful chance to develop emotionally as well as spiritually.

Here are a few suggestions to make use of the energy of the full moon to attract good luck into your lives:

Offer blessings to all who are in need. Since the power of the full moon is in your favor it is possible to offer the love and light to your colleagues, friends as well as family members and friends together with forgiveness as well as the healing power. It is also possible to send peace energies out to those which might be undergoing the hardships of war, poverty or tension. You will be able to provide them with many benefits, as well as generating the perfect opportunity for Karma. A full moon in the middle of the month is a great time to show compassion and give back towards others.

Meditate. If you pray, you speak to your god. While you are meditating and pray, you allow these gods to communicate with you. Relax in the glow of the moon and breathe deeply. Take for as long as you can handle it, and take all the connections to energy, wisdom, and the flow of energy which are flying across the universe towards you. As the moon's fullness gives the energy of a full moon and energy, it's important to find peace, calm and harmony. It can be accomplished by yourself or in a space that is sacred.

There is the possibility of connecting to your friends, or even an entire group. There is a chance to locate a religious center and yoga studio as well as an groups online that meet to meditate on the full moon. This can be extremely beneficial meditation in the company of others. The tides of the ocean are at their highest at this time so your tide will rise as well. It is important to utilize this to receive these messages, or else they'll appear to be passing through your ears.

Visualize your dreams being manifested. When the moon is full, it's an ideal time to practice methods to manifest. Spend time time to think about your dreams and note them down on the paper. This is also an excellent time to examine the vision board to determine whether you require any adjustments.

You must ensure that the vision board you have created is somewhere you are able to see it each day. Make time to take the time to concentrate on your desires at night for an additional push.

Keep your thoughts optimistic. We all know that we must keep our thoughts positive as frequently as is possible in the full moon, so that you enjoy the wind on your back. Positive thoughts are multiplied and you feel more energized. In the event that you only make a few minutes following your awake and just before going to the bed, to consider your positive experiences and the blessings that you are blessed with within your life and you'll be doing an excellent job for yourself and your life. It is possible to write an appreciation checklist.

It is possible to write your Universe an appreciation note to thank you for the gifts you've received. Check yourself in the mirror, and affirm yourself with nice words. Take a stroll and take in all the beautiful things all around yourself. Think about how your positive thoughts may were sprinkled by the glimmer of the moon's fullness to allow them to grow more expansive.

Do not get upset or fight. It is important to remain at peace when the moon is full. It is important to forgive people and take a deep breath during the difficult times, and let the negative be. If you aren't able to let the things go, it is important to share them with other people. It is best to put off discussing the things that have upset you until after the full moon has gone away for 2 days. Things that occur in this time is multiplied. It's like fertilizing your emotional state. Maintain your enthusiasm towards a positive, joyful direction, whether in your vehicle, at work at home, or every day interactions.

Family and Friends Bonfire. Play the drums with someone Be present, take a deep breath and move around the heat of the flame. It was said by an old timer that spirits perceive you better through the glowing light of a fireplace So make sure that you're paving the way for your guides from the spirit world to come across you, so they are able to send them their messages. Be sure that you're prepared and open to receiving the message.

Release and the Waning Moon. Similar to the moon that waxes it will also be three moons that wane throughout the month of April. All of us will support you towards surrendering and dissolving the plans of the Universe and your destiny.

Waning Crescent The Waning Crescent is the most waning phase in the moon's cycle, and offers the lowest frequency. It is possible to feel tired and exhausted, however that's totally normal in this time. The goal of this phase is to rest and recover because you've gotten rid of items that are hindering you. Although it's normal to experience fatigue however, it's equally important to let go of any emotions you are experiencing.

Take a look, feel them, repair them, and get moving. Your goal is to achieve your potential and this will require certain hard choices and effort.

Chapter 12: The Eight Phases Of The Moon

"I observe the moon and the moon also sees my." The women of the world have for centuries enjoyed a strong bond to the moon. They seek their mystic powers as well as guidance and focus. They yearn for it as do other people who yearn for the sun to come out.

The moon's presence can make us feel strong. It gives us strength and vitality by the moon's presence. It's just a matter of learning how to be a part of each lunar phase.

The moon is regarded as feminine in the an astrological sense. The moon is our governing force for monthly cycle, our emotions, and fertility. Every female may be influenced by her influence. The pull recedes, then renews as the waves.

It is a feeling that we are attracted to between periods of introversion and contemplation, and it is not uncommon to experience moments of intense enthusiasm and energy.

It is a fact that history has proven how much influence the moon has over us. The term "lunatic" is derived from a number of diverse languages, which refer to the condition of hysteria, or even madness. It comes from the Latin term "lunaticus," that originally was a reference to epilepsy and madness due to the belief that diseases are caused by the moon. as well as from "monseoc," the Old English "monseoc," "lunatic" literally means "moon-sick."

Pliny the Elder is the Roman historian as well as Aristotle The Greek philosopher believed that as the brain is an organ that's "moist" and that our minds can be influenced by moon's pull, just like tides.

Ujjwal Chakraborty explains in his article, The Impacts of the Different Phases of Lunar Moon on Humans that a variety of research studies have revealed an association with lunar phases and human reproduction patterns, as well as the pattern in physical activities, illnesses physical and psychological well-being.

Elizabeth Palermo found a similarity between the two words "month" in addition to "moon" can't be an accident.

Each moon phase is a different one: the last quarter, the first quarter, and the new one; all occur once time each month. Scientifically speaking the reason for these changes is because of how far between sun and moon and the amount of light reflect back onto the moon by the Earth.

The moon takes about 29 and a half hours to travel around the Earth and, during the full orbit, it is possible to observe each moon phase. Every phase takes place approximately 7.4 days from each other.

There is a special spiritual significance and energy at the root of every single phase. Scientists can provide some explanations.

However, the rest are areas the ones where experience, faith and faith assume the role of.

The way they live their lives according to lunar calendars has held special significance to women, since we're both emotionally and physically following the identical times. If the moon must change its direction, retract and then gradually receding every month, we must as well. The human experience is a journey through diverse emotional states exactly the similar way that the moon revolves around the Earth. The more attuned our bodies are with the various phases and how they impact our lives, we are able to channel those energies instead of fighting the effects of them.

New Beginnings New Moon

Spiritually, the new moons symbolize the cycle of menstruation for women. through the ages, women were apart from others in this time.

Do not think of the moon's new phase as a chance to start fresh, instead, it's as a time to rest. In this time it is a chance to start fresh and build your confidence. New beginnings, clean slates as well as new beginnings accompany the moon's new phase. It is important to take advantage of this time for "reboot".

Imagine the "battery" becoming recharged with the rays of the new moon. Get rid of all the clutter and thoughts to the side.

For this to happen do this, you must unplug yourself from the world and enjoy the time to enjoy some time on your own. It is possible that you will be withdrawn and unsocial. Check for any of these symptoms and then embrace these feelings.

If the moon is turning her dark side to us, remove yourself from those who drain your energy, and focus on your own. Don't feel guilty if you must cancel plans because it isn't your intention to be answering the phone or hang in the company of others.

Tuning out and turning off is the most effective option to survive the night of a new moon.

Scientifically speaking: The new moon is born in the moment that the moon and sun coincide on the opposite sides of the earth. Because the sun doesn't face the moon's direction, when we look at Earth it appears as it's its dark moon was in our direction.

Setting Intentions Waxing Crescent

Spiritually: This period of the moon is a time to make wishes aspirations, hope, and desires. After you recharged your batteries with the moon's new light all your hopes and desires are now in place.

It's the time that you should develop your goals, set the foundation to begin your next venture Make checks payable for the Universe and then bury your crystals.

Scientifically speaking: As the moon is moving closer to the sun, it starts to lighten. The moon will observe a crescent. Less than half the moon's light is illuminated until it becomes larger or gets into the initial quarter.

Action First Quarter Moon

Spiritually: Because this first full moon takes place just one week following New Moon, it is the time when we start to encounter resistance from obstructions. If you set intentions prior to the new moon, you'll be faced with your first setbacks. Decisions, actions, and difficulties will be encountered in this time.

The time of making plans and resting is over and you must do more. Prepare the ability to take decisions fast and keep your cool If things come from the midst of your thoughts.

The most effective way to handle the moon the ability to change. Set your goals for the moon's new phase in your thoughts all time. You must ensure that any decisions you take will result in you the desired outcome.

The most effective way to start doing something about them is to write them down in a journal. Write down your thoughts and then act upon your plans. Write down a daily schedule of items you have to complete and then mark them off when you accomplish each day.

Scientifically, the moon will enter its first quarter about a week following the first moon. This is referred to as the first quarter as the moon has reached just one quarter to the month's phase.

Refine Waxing Gibbous

Spiritually: Refinement, editing adjustments and editing are commonplace around the moon in this time. The things don't always go as we'd desired, and this moon's phase may let you know which areas you should change the direction of your life, abandon on or reconsider.

If you'd like to enjoy the full benefits that come with a full moon you may be required to compromise some aspects. It could be necessary to alter the direction you take.

Don't be afraid of the feeling of the need to change in this stage.

Scientifically speaking: The waxing moon is only one step away from turning into an full moon. The moon is easily visible in the daylight since it has a large part that is illuminating.

Harvest Full Moon

Spiritually: Because the sun and the moon lie located on opposite sides of the Earth and are located in opposite zodiac signs as well. This could create more tension since we're trying to strike a middle ground between the extremes.

The emotions will be high at the time. It's important not to become terribly connected or emotionally to something in this time.

The moon's first full moon in September is known as the Harvest Moon.

It is also the time where farmers are able to take their harvests. As they reap the rewards of the seeds that were put in earlier in the year it is your responsibility to ensure that you are benefiting from all of the advantages that come from the intentions you have set at the time of the new moon.

The benefits you've earned could manifest as the result of all of the work you've put into it. These benefits could manifest as opportunities that aren't there yet. You must be willing and ready to take advantage of these opportunities.

The scientifically-based explanation for a full moon is that it is in the event that the sun and moon reside on opposite side of Earth. Because the sun is just across the moon, its sunlight is illuminating it totally. The moon appears as full when you view it through the Earth.

Grateful Waning Gibbous

Spiritually: Joy, enthusiasm shared, gratitude, and sharing will be the theme of this moon period. The moon should be feeling all your benefits from the effort you've made in the last two weeks. You're "crops" are numerous and you'll be able to see certain, even though they're not huge, results that are a result of your goals and the intentions you've established.

This is the time to be filled with affection. It is your desire to be a blessing to your loved ones.

It is possible to treat your spouse to a night with friends. It is possible to buy your friend an item since you spotted something which brought you back to their name.

It is possible that you will spend on more this week that you typically would. Be careful not to go overboard with the spending, but don't feel poor about how much you paid for the people that who you love. Giving back is the primary focus during this time.

Scientifically: When the full moon has gone it begins to become less bright. The moon dims towards the final quarter moon before returning to a full moon.

Release Last Quarter

Spiritually Let go, forgiveness and freedom surround the moon at this time. Like the moon shrinking, so do it is important to prepare to let go of things. Through the month, you could be angry, hurt or injured.

In this period of the moon it is the time when you are able to let go of all the frustration and anger. The need to clean your own self in order to be able to accept the goals you'll given during the next new moon.

One of the best practices during this period is cleaning. Clear out your closets examine your relationships and tidy up your home. Find anything that's not useful to you and throw the items out.

Look out for any emotional and physical clutter has accumulated in your previous phases, and then remove the clutter. To get rid of this emotional burden, engage in any fitness activity you are enjoying.

Scientifically, this phase of the moon's phase is total reverse of the previous quarter when it begins the transition to a full moon. Following a full moon the moon's brightness will decrease and become smaller. The moon will turn into a gibbous moon. It then moves in the final quarter.

Surrender Waning Crescent

Spiritually: Rest, recuperate and let go. There is a possibility that you feel completely exhausted in this time. You've been through an entire moon cycle and you have experienced a variety of events.

Perhaps you have let things go or received something. It is possible that you have voluntarily accepted or let things go, or you could have been fighting certain items. There is a need to plan for the new moon and an upcoming cycle. There is nothing wrong with setting goals, but only during the current phase.

In the moment, you have to let go of the Universe and let it go. There are things that will always to happen that are beyond your hands and destiny is going been allowed to play its game.

Scientifically: The final part of moon which is lit down is becoming smaller, and on the path to becoming an upcoming moon.

www.ingramcontent.com/pod-product-compliance
Lightning Source LLC
Chambersburg PA
CBHW071444080526
44587CB00014B/1986